ISN'T IT ROMANTIC

100 LOVE POEMS BY YOUNGER AMERICAN POETS

ISN'T IT ROMANTIC

100 LOVE POEMS BY YOUNGER AMERICAN POETS

♥ ♥ ♥ ♥ ♥ ♥ ♥ ♥ ♥ ♥ ♥

EDITED BY BRETT FLETCHER LAUER & AIMEE KELLEY

WITH AN INTRODUCTION

BY CHARLES SIMIC

VERSE PRESS

AMHERST, MASSACHUSETTS

Published by Verse Press
www.versepress.org

Please see full acknowledgments at the back of this book.

Library of Congress Cataloging-in-Publication Data

Isn't it romantic : 100 love poems by younger American poets / edited by Brett Fletcher Lauer & Aimee Kelley ; introduction by Charles Simic.-- 1st ed.
    p. cm.
  ISBN 0-9746353-1-6 (pbk. with audio cd : alk. paper)
  1. Love poetry, American. I. Lauer, Brett Fletcher. II. Kelley, Aimee.
  PS595.L6I84 2004
  811'.540803543--dc22

                    2004012537

Available to the trade through Consortium Book Sales and Distribution, 1045 Westgate Drive, St. Paul, Minnesota 55114.

Cover Art: Alexa Horochowski, detail from "Mary and Joseph." Used by permission of the artist.

Book & CD design by J. Johnson
Text set in Adobe Caslon Regular. Display set in Adobe Caslon SC and Knockout.
Printed in the United States of America

9 8 7 6 5 4 3 2 1

First Edition

for you

CONTENTS

Introduction

I Love You Baby Till Cows Come Home

> I had no
> idea
> what to do
> with the word
>
> "she"; now it seems
> like I don't know
> any other
> word. . . .

> -Aaron Kunin

I recall fondly that the subject of my first sleepless nights as a very young boy was a girl on my street I was in love with. I lay awake trying to imagine what was under her prim little dress. When a few years later in high school I came to write my first love poems, I had such reveries to serve me as material. All of a sudden, I had to find words for the erotic images in my mind. It all had to be subtle, relying on innuendoes and a bit of Romantic rhetoric to make it appetizing to the object of my affection. Of course, there was no guarantee. Love is blind, so a poem written in that condition is often sappy or downright moronic. After all, how many ways are there to describe someone's lips, eyes and hair? What would be worse than to hear the one you adore burst out laughing while reading the poem? No wonder so many of our great American poets hardly wrote any love poems. They feared making fools of themselves. They were right. Whoever sets out to write about love is taking the biggest risk of his or her life.

I once asked a rowdy, tough-looking class of New York City high school students what they thought about poetry. They couldn't believe I was asking such a stupid question. Poetry sucks, they told me one and all. Okay, I said, what about love notes. Don't you slip love notes to one another? Nobody said anything to that, but a number of them had their heads lowered in shame and one or two were even blushing. That led to my next question: What about love poems? Do you write them? Again, there was a silence, but I could see I had perked up their interest. To my shock, a boy raised his hand and volunteered to read a love poem he had written. What made it even more astonishing is the teacher had warned me that this particular kid was nothing but trouble. He stood in front of the class with a tiny piece of notebook paper and read to us some sentimental rhymed mush which after a few snickers was received with moist-eyed attention by the girls and grudging respect by the other roughnecks.

As the ancients already realized, love poetry is the only type of poetry that can be put into practical use. You wrote this for me? The one you fancy exclaims. Yes, you admit shyly, even though you may have used the poem—with a few details altered—to seduce other women. What you expect from the poem is nothing short of a miracle: spirit becoming flesh; words becoming deeds; the two of you hopping into bed. The existence of a long tradition of poetry on the amorous shenanigans of lovers confirms my thesis. It is conclusive evidence that human beings think as much about love and sex as they do about their gods.

Isn't It Romantic: 100 Love Poems by Younger American Poets is an astonishing revelation. How could so many poems about love be so inventive and so good? I'm impressed by the anthropological zeal and critical acumen of the editors. They have uncovered what we didn't know existed. A hundred poets writing about love in a country in which most news nowadays is about violence, death and destruction, is cause for joy. The poems in the anthology are varied, nicely-written, clever, funny, sexy and always entertaining. "Happiness is by its nature inexpressible," Octavio Paz said. Almost three thousand years ago, Sappho wrote that she found it more thrilling to watch her girlfriend take off her skirt than to see the Greek fleet or the Trojan cavalry getting themselves ready for battle. Anyone reading this anthology is bound to arrive at the same conclusion.

Charles Simic

ISN'T IT ROMANTIC

Joshua Beckman

Don't be mad,
I'm in bed thinking
of you at work.

Josh Bell

Poem to Line My Casket with, Ramona

Come practice your whorish gestures in the graveyard, Ramona.
Come sharpen your teeth on the tombstones.
Cough up the roots if you know what's good for you.
When coyotes are teaching their young to howl,
ghoulies rehearse the Courtship of Wristbones.
When you hear clawing at the square of styrofoam
serving as a window in the caretaker's shack,
then you must count each step going up to the mausoleum,
and my ghost will appear in the churchyard.
He'll kiss the back of your knee in the moonlight.
These are not promises, but eerie enough, regardless.
You must count out loud, Ramona, the steps,
because this is the time to watch what eats you.
I used to love the way the wind whistled through your teeth
when you drove the back roads, above your legal limit.
I used to have these poses. They turned into habits.
I used to love the folks that loved me.
And they've been sad ones, my years since being dead.
And they've been coming, the folks who claim to love me.
And I hardly recognize myself. There aren't mirrors, as such.
The drum section rattles it out, down by the high school.
I hear them, or is it the caretaker drunk in his wheelbarrow?
You used to play the wheelbarrow, I recall.
You used to wash your underwear in the sink.
Above ground, the wind whistles through the tombstones.
Below ground, the wind sleeps and has colors.
Below ground, colors are how I dream of making my comeback.
There's a difference between *a* white dress and *the* white dress.
You used to strip off *the* white dress in a highly professional manner.
You used to dangle the remote, and I'd come get it.
You used to skip church. You used to skip dinner parties.
Now you've been seen hoisting condoms from the pharmacy.
There are twelve condoms to a pack. A pack of lovers mills outside your door.

A pack of the dead are heading toward the showers.
A pack of dead lovers is referred to as "a creep" of dead lovers.
More than one dead lover is weeping. But oh, how it was me who loved
  you then.
You with your cracked lips, with your love and your other defilements
  kept alive in a bucket.
When I first died, I stole a lock of your hair while you slept.
Now I dip it in ink when the mood strikes,
and the times you visit and kneel so pretty on the grass above me,
that's not scratching you hear. It's writing.

David Berman

CLASSIC WATER

I remember Kitty saying we shared a deep longing for
the consolation prize, laughing as we rinsed the stagecoach.

I remember the night we camped out
      and I heard her whisper
"think of me as a place" from her sleeping bag
      with the centaur print.

I remember being in her father's basement workshop
when we picked up an unknown man sobbing
over the shortwave radio

and the night we got so high we convinced ourselves
that the road was a hologram projected by the headlight beams.

I remember how she would always get everyone to vote
on what we should do next and the time she said
"all water is classic water" and shyly turned her face away.

At volleyball games her parents sat in the bleachers
like ambassadors from Indiana in all their midwestern schmaltz.

She was destroyed when they were busted for operating
a private judicial system within U.S. borders.

Sometimes I'm awakened in the middle of the night
by the clatter of a room service cart and I think back on Kitty.

Those summer evenings by the government lake,
talking about the paradox of multiple Santas
or how it felt to have your heart broken.

I still get a hollow feeling on Labor Day when the summer ends

and I remember how I would always refer to her boyfriends
as what's-his-face, which was wrong of me and I'd like
to apologize to those guys right now, wherever they are:

No one deserves to be called what's-his-face.

Anselm Berrigan

THE VARIOUS MULTITUDES CONTAINED BY THE LOVES OF MY LOVE

& I've always admired fiction but I've never admired the fiction
that is on the swing in the warehouse kicking paint cans & I
double pumped so collapse went my young robot companion &
a polaroid snapped history into our lives & white energy escaped
through the hole in my foot which I acquired by stepping on a nail
after a great jump I got off quick but my lover was out of town
& my lover is depressed & my lover in a foreign land can't sleep
& I am counted out of my fiction & I have no lovers though I love
my lovers & I have no lovers but I love them & they love to be happy
& they love to be sleepy & they love to be chased by their numbers
& I love to understand ones now & I love to understand zeros now
& I look forward to sleeping on mud & I love to give my blanket
which asks for nothing to my host & I love to imitate my lovers &
I love to ignore the crosses in my kitchen & I love to swing when
the ball is in the glove & I love to send messages to my love & I love
to check the voice mail for messages from my love & I love the shoulders
& the space between them that is love & love & love & the whatness
of the space in my love goes to hell & the it of my love goes to lunch
& my love is an object with great use of verbs & my love is an object
with great use of colors & I love to know that objects are absolutely
amazing now & the mud of the love I love is incredible love & Larry
Eigner is love & copping some love is proof of further love & here
comes love talking a lot & the last thing you can do is intentionally
walk love & love takes its pants off & lies on the lawn under a brown
& grey sunset & love sits on the couch in its underwear & love has
a package taped to its leg & inside the package is a note from my love
& I read it loving to understand that I've been hopelessly defeated
by love

Edmund Berrigan

THE HISTORY OF THE HUMAN BODY

You're so yourself sometimes I'm sure it's you
in front of me & not the nothing I have use
to see or that mostly I'm looking for like looking
& waiting to be that other. Clarity & perfection
are like, of no use to an incomplete mind, mind
killed to prove the other, that is our beauty.
I can't see you but I can see myself wanting
you, to write that down, which I have done in
the past & had you more in front of me. You had
just been there, it had been hours, & your
energy is bright a hundred feet away, that its
image is strongly etched years later, making itself
my double between this double couch & coffee
table, good for any moment I want to see you.

Mark Bibbins

By the Skin of Our Luck

I used to ride around in the hole
in your lapel. From there I could watch

the fires climb out of the dumpsters
and into the sky while you caught

cinders on your tongue like snow.
I felt safe when I figured out

what you actually wanted,
despite the odd aerosol can

exploding in the night behind us
and the pleasure of your hand

sometimes finding me though otherwise
you let me pretend I was hidden.

The sun followed us all the way
to Mallorca, as did the lone helicopter

that trails me to this day.
I don't even hear it anymore

but I see what it does to the surface
of the water and your hair

and I'm sorry—you thought it was
your fault, didn't you, all those years.

Brian Blanchfield

THE ENDOWMENT BECOMING LESS AN INSTITUTION

The Endowment for Long Mornings in Bed
would like to recognize your continued contributions to wonder, at large,
and, for the project outlined in your proposal to get two glasses
of ice water from the kitchen, is pleased to grant a day's residency
in warm covers. Generous Endowment. A stretch.

I see you have seen another room. Its freshening finishes.
The freezer is sad, come back.
The day we don't fail doesn't miss us.
Think of the best parts of *The Rainbow*.

I was thinking the honeymoon, the embryonic swim out of time.
But will one of us build a church on the premises and say, as you say,
For both of us? I see it is me. A highmindedness the world
would only ground. Some air. Yes, have some space.
I will not frame arches, say enter.
The water is perfect in its own way, and your pillow is my pillow.

Lee Ann Brown

AFTER SAPPHO

So many people
advised me against you.
How glad I am
we could not resist.

Oni Buchanan

The Only Yak in Batesville, Virginia

At first I spent hours gazing at the black and white horse
in the farthest pasture. He was so far away,
so tiny between the fence slats, and even then I knew
all he cared about was his mane and that his tail
was properly braided. He never so much as galloped
in my direction. Even the flies that edged
his beautiful eyes never flew into my wool
or landed on my nose. The love affair

was over before it began. I started to dream
of a dry cistern in the middle of the forest
and dry leaves where the other yaks could play
until leaves stuck out of their hair and they looked
like shrubs. In my dream they lived
in the cistern and each morning looked out
with periscopes before scrambling up the concrete walls
to search in the forest for sprouting trees.

In winter I realized that for the other yaks
it was fall all year round, and that it had to be fall,
because otherwise they couldn't roll in the leaves
to look like shrubs, and there had to be a cistern,
because otherwise they couldn't huddle in the pitch black,
and I knew then that I had forgotten
what a yak looks like, though I am a yak,
and I knew then that I had been away for a long time.

Stephen Burt

A Sudden Rain in the Green Mountains
for Jessica Bennett

Plush hills, the raw materials, fall away.

The soaking clay

In which the serried oaks, the picturesque

And swaybacked pines, elected to evolve,

The famous marble in its bare reserve,

Vanish like guesses in these verticals

Whose heft at dusk

Blurs rooks to ridges, veils the bicycles

And splashes where they lean hard into curves.

Looming like crowds, such weather makes its world;

Its crash and draft and spate and uniform

Consonant force confirm

Or mean—not that without you there are no

Attainments I can care for or call good—

But that among them, missing you, I know

How much delight, green need

And weird vivacious luck drew me to you:

Luck lasts with us. Out here I can believe

That all companionships only rehearse

Or faintly copy ours, and make it plain—

As over the plain inn, the plain roof clears—

That granite, marble, nascent evening stars

And that impressive dinner bell, the moon,

Still seem—may seem, to me, forever-yours,

A portraitist's surround to set you off

For admiration and comparison.

In light you spare, unevenly, they shine

To give such thought, your thought, occasion,

Triangulate, and show me where you are.

I'm not with you. I will be with you soon.

Garrett Caples

Targets and Flowers (Begun with Lines from Breton)

Sometimes she turns around in the printed seasons and asks the time, or even pretends to look jewels straight in the eye.

Sometimes she gets her bearings from watchmakers, her hardness from the balance-beam, as she bends to pull a stocking up.

Sometimes she glances into mirrors, impressing onto unglazed surfaces imaged permanence.

Sometimes she appears in the center of something circular—targets and flowers—and hurriedly adjusts her hair.

Sometimes she speaks in mascara.

Sometimes she clasps an hourglass between her legs and slows time to a trickling waltz, or writes her signature across an hour's measure.

Sometimes, when she's "in vogue," she walks abroad in search of the *Herald-Tribune,* and people throw coins and gum and fruit, mistaking her for the Russian dancer with the wintry smile and clandestine desires.

Sometimes she removes the flares from the modern mode, and brings forth objects stout and stiffened with stove-enamel.

Sometimes she reverses the tweedle and tintinnabulation into a giddy spiral of music, translating somersaults with a turn of the lathe into smooth and careless gestures.

Sometimes she sparks these gyrations.

Robert N. Casper

UNTITLED

Remember our ecstatic parade,
How we gathered ourselves for each other?
We went beyond the ruins of youth
And the dreamland where thieves lie in wait—
Out to where our sighs
Were a kind of unanswerable question.
There our thingness split apart
Till we fit the shape of each moment,
As nuthatch bedevils titmouse
And earthworm slithers through loam.

Michael Earl Craig

Good Night, Star

You can't step out of your tragedy, it wouldn't be a tragedy.
Neither can I.
Together we walk

and think thoughts in a cornfield.
I take my blue pencil, snap in half my blue pencil.
A thing cries out from the interior of Corn.

A thing cries but nothing rises as a crow.
You light my cigarettes, I smoke two
at a time. I lay back on the tractor

staring up at the sky.
I stare up through you
into the backside of the cosmos, the backlit

blaze of the backside
where a clean-shaven God untangles two lampcords.
That's what one eye does.

The other trails off with the comet.
I am tired and full of sloth, you
have just shown me this.

I look a bobwhite in the eye.
A kind of insect bounces off my forehead.
I feel almost put here to lean up against a tree.

Am I whole, dear star?
As my eyelashes grow down
to the ground might you braid them?

Caroline Crumpacker

TRANS-RELATIONAL LOVE POEM

You are
      walking up the stairs
        of a clear glass building

designed
for the repetition
      of sensation.

When you reach the fourth floor,
      enter.

There is the boudoir en pleine aire.
There are your countless abilities.
There is the Romantic Empire
      throwing off the Classical Empire.

So step up.

The architects are playing with your vertigo.
They are playing with your need to be inside.
They are playing with the idea that
      one cannot rub one's shoes
      on a work of art.

How many of the senses are aroused?

Does it depend on the architectural model

      or

on the perfumerie of the lady of the house.

Perfume, like architecture, is designed
for the repetition of sensation

as a means of variance.

Playing with the definition of sensation.
Playing with the definition
of romance.
Playing on the glass floors
with ballet slippers
visible throughout the quarter.

And everywhere,
the influence of mortality.

And everywhere,
the sensation of interiority.

And everywhere
a valentine for the invisible

playing with the idea of the beloved
playing a music
the likes of this building:

meaning height

not dependent
on the idea of height

but repeating it
in unlikely configurations.

Meaning

a friendly psychoanalysis
of its own powers,

as

in romance
as the only definition of romance.

SELF PORTRAIT IN HORSE HAIR WIG

In the Next Life in an absinthe slip
Of ribbons, water-silk coat, glass seeds
Like water at the throat, I'll be adored
By a kneeling army of boys.
In a Blue-Blood summer, you'll be criminal:
Clyde-like, dark-eyed and timid.
Your face will be of brilliant countenance.
There will be no dour consequence to our secret
Meeting. In the evening, we will be astonishing-
As-ever in perfect dress, minds spinning
With whirlwind of the world's questions.
In a room of hard-pasted porcelain and water-clocks,
You'll press your slender fingers at the hinge,
Discover a hidden winter trapped in a snuffbox.

Tenaya Darlington

Field Guide to Western Intimacy

1. Select a clean surface, avoiding dirt and litter.

2. Preparations for mounting should start immediately, in the field.

3. Sprinkle water on work space and lay the body "show-side" down.

4. Here is a list of suggested tools: a curved grapefruit knife, a small ruler, spirits, mixing bowls, pliers, backing, a hair dryer, dowel rods, white shellac.

5. Beauty is largely water. Shrunken areas may develop as time passes.

6. The next obstacle to be encountered will be the wings.

7. Virginity represents purity of one who lives far from corruption, close to animals.

8. Disjoint this hinge.

9. If in doubt as to the legality or propriety of lovemaking, consult a warden.

10. Your holiness is the answer to every question ever asked.

11. When your will is boundless, the skin breaks free.

Cort Day

Once As Thoth Beside The Sea

Once when I was Thoth
and in Thoth's ibis head,
she knelt beside me
in the sand, wearing only
a too-small negligee
in whose edges the ocean
fluttered and burned.
Because an ibis has an eye
on each side, she was
constantly bifurcating,
and I was having some trouble
with depth perception,
so while I put on her blindfold,
she waited patiently,
shivering in my left eye.
We wanted to record
the absorption spectra
of three surfaces:
the ocean, her, and me.
It worked like a charm.
The data gave us cause
for celebration: the sea
was hopelessly out of tune,
but I was degenerate
in only one lobe, and she
had no internal bleeding
to speak of. The weight
removed, we repaired
to our motel room,
while behind us the ocean,
that cauldron of gases,
continued to expound
its theories of love.

Mónica de la Torre

DRIVEN BY A STRANGE DESIRE

I. Before Breakfast

When the sun turns gray and I become tired
of looking at your many-colored shoes

I will give you balloons for all the holes
we speak too much to fill. Who believes

in air, nowadays? Or do you prefer tea
with the dried fruit I will have to throw out

the window of your room? Because I want
this to stop I want this to stop I want this

II. Towards Moorish Spain

To kill the dragons is a different thing
in my family there are only lizards.

In Sevilla—never famous for its lamps—
a dissected crocodile hangs from a ceiling.

The reptile, the Crown's Bizantine gift. Its teeth
suspended in the air of the cathedral.

I stole a pair of shoes, but didn't run far
from the orchard where water had women's scent.

Thirst is not fear, thirst is not green, but has wings
like dragons, or airplanes. As oranges

in Sevilla, driven by a strange desire
to stay where they are. Floating. Suspended.

III. Towards Virgo

The Milky Way is not only expanding;
the Bang is not only a Bang. It is drifting

and being pulled away from, let's say, something.
Because dark matter is ninety nine of what

there is and visible matter is so small
it clusters together and forms a Great Wall.

China and Spain and my eyes reading the paper.
We are still together, are we not, wondering if.

Timothy Donnelly

Isn't It Romantic?

His thought appalled us. It bore the mark of having strayed too deep into
the company of others. And what a drastic forest that is. Larchwood,
leaf mold, *ignis fatuus;* bandit faces grazing on him on an antique train.
And he allows it, yes. Allows each mouth its history of twisting, allows
each fist. It's much too hideous to dwell on, sadly. *Only ten more minutes,*
he thought, *and I'll be lying softly in my rented dark, almost invisible.* Well,
you can see it, can't you—how it bears the mark? He absolutely should
have put it this way: "Only ten minutes more…." And what does it
mean, that he'll be lying "softly"? We are all of us liars, and we doubt
it means anything, anything at all. He has fallen into a habit we abhor,
as one might fall from a hotel window ten flights up, the darker throes
of rapture, bathrobed. And he has landed "softly" in the crowded bed
of a passing truck. (We'll show him "softly.") The truck barrels off.
"Crowded" with what is what you want to know. Well, Inspector, that
would have to be manikins. Hairless limbs and paint expressions, some
kept whole but most disconnected, all of them naked with the stink of
plastic. And look at him scramble just to keep them warm, as if it could
matter! (Let's suppose it's snowing.) And when he realizes that he can't
save all, he chooses one. She's still intact, though her look is distant. He
dresses her up in his hotel robe; he belts it tight. Isn't it romantic? He
throws his useless arms around her, throws his worries into her empty
head. If you could just for once. (It's forever, get it?) If you could just for
once keep your damned trap shut. Isn't it romantic? He chooses one; he
belts it tight. The truck barrels off into an endless night. If you could just
for once. No one ever talks to us the way he talks; just listen to him coo:
"You want me to clear out room for you to sleep in? You want me to see
to it nobody touches you?"

Ben Doyle

An Error of the Hydrographers

But you are so thin,
you're not even part
of this room. We had
us a bonfire, all
your frames we could find.
Our firepit must have
been built over a
groundwasp's hive, they came
out angry, aflame,
flying. They didn't know
we were there.

              Some dropped
back in. You named them
part of your picture.
I said your name. I
was so close but then
I was inside you.

Marcella Durand

Reading Postures 3

this sort of position uncomfortable allows me to speak
more comfortably with you, the one I love, this placement
of arms upon legs and cheeks upon mouths, and tumbled
together like clothes in a dryer, gives a permission as free
as a dog in a park, or picking up a hand and letting it
drop away, and then grabbing it again, tight enough to
feel all the extremities & the weather changes, while draped
over two beings think of several more and not just positions
but locale, as of this writing, we can think of several more
museums with exhibitions of bodies in just about every
sort of posture, and while admiring their spines, one eye
wanders off, as the french say, to check out the small lake
shimmering off thru the artificial ballrooms & bedrooms &
rooms of reception & even the small shopfront hidden away
here down this hallway, ripped off during some war and brought
over in pieces, just like the multistory wooden lattice stolen from
a church, whether it was bought, stolen & tossed on waves
like matchsticks, like wood, with gilded corners and eggshell
touches and the artist's name hidden somewhere like a tattoo
somewhere on your body, some unexplored fold, some intrusion
of ink & spray, some artist touched you before I touched you,
some boat brought you over the waters.

Atomic Bride
for Andre Foxxe

A good show
Starts in the
Dressing room

And works its way
To the stage.
Close the door,

Andre's cross-
dressing, what
a drag. All

The world loves
A bride, something
About those gowns.

A good wedding
Starts in the
Department store

And works its way
Into the photo album.
Close the door,

Andre's tying
The knot, what
A drag. Isn't he

Lovely? All
The world loves
A bachelor, some-

thing about glamour
& glitz, white
Shirts, lawsuits.

A good dog
Starts in the yard
And works its way

Into da house.
Close your eyes.
Andre's wide open,

One freak of the week
Per night, what
A drag. Isn't

He lovely? All
The world loves
A nuclear family,

Something about
A suburban home,
Chaos in order.

A good bride starts
In the laboratory
And works his way

To the church.
Close the door,
Andre's thinking

Things over, what
A drag. Isn't
He lovely? All

The world loves
A divorce, something
About broken vows.

A good war starts
In the courtroom
And works its way

To the album cover.
Close the door,
Andre's swearing in,

What a drag.
Isn't he lovely? All
The world loves

A star witness,
something about
Cross-examination.

A good drug starts
In Washington
And works its way

To the dance floor.
Close the door,
Andre's strung-out,

What a drag.
Isn't he lovely? All
The world loves

Rhythm guitar,
Something about
Those warm chords.

A good skeleton
Starts in the closet
And works its way

To the top of the charts.
Start the organ.
Andre's on his way

Down the aisle,
Alone, what an encore. All
The world loves

An explosive ending.
Go ahead Andre,
Toss the Bouquet.

Monica Ferrell

The King With His Queen

My victory, my triumph, my memory, my fabulous
Speed, my kingdom, my forest fire, my pure
Flashflood in a thimble. My morning orison,
My dovecote, my insurrection, my soaked
Bales of hay, my great bane. Throbbing, ruinous thing
You scent of autumn and its dark bowl, whose waters

Brim over everything and change it all to bone. My
Excellent marksman, my kennels guard who feeds the starving
Scores and plucks out their motes—
They blink and, overcome by gratefulness,
Say nothing, just like your hands, my sister
In hospice, at midnight with black dress trailing.

Let me tell you your funeral in the pewter rain
Was like holding my breath and with quiet tread
Following into the room where you were
Dressing, vapor in the old blind mirror. Love,
All the messages brought down by your gold-
Throated angels have come out garbled and rot,

Tell me one five-letter-word how I may survive
This era of red leaves, the poaching season
Without my Chief of the Hunt. Without my legion,
My bowl of ocean, my delicious crystal
Chess-piece who always captured her beleaguered king.
You were my lake's smile as it rises out of darkness

Under the burgeoning stars—and still, my candelabra's
One stubborn wick: when all the porters are down the hall dozing
And the castle hardens into a hard knot of blood
Aching to pass through the contracted valve—you are
The dance of shadows in the drunken room
And its invitation with outstretched fingers.

THE COMPASS ROOM: EAST

Each book has a title and all chapters have numbers and each page has a number and each paragraph begins with a clear indentation, a pause or a clearing of a throat, and each sentence ends with a period and each word ends with a sound and each time we meet has the allure of progress away from something medieval such as violent unpaved roads and bawdy unplucked fowl running amok in the uncleared fields at the outer regions of fiefdoms. We congregate in dinners that are literate and referential, to books, to other people, to friends who favor not being there, knowing that we will speak about them lovingly yet with candor, sudden intonations of confession, unfounded opinions, half-truths, to oblige their spirits and to position ourselves nicely for the future, carving out trenches and borderlines that can be bent later, but not broken, when we ourselves choose to be absent. The noise of the news comes over the radio while someone has put a tape on the stereo, fusing a concert of musical effort and topical events beneath the chop chop of the vegetables and the scraping of nerves which run along the legs of chairs and pass into the doorbell, ringing as we all arrive.

We are all in love. Or we wouldn't be friends. At some point we have each of us pressed earnest notes into soaked winter pockets, or sat on the porches of houses at the latest hours of evening, leaning back into shadows and sharing a cigarette while someone who should be listening is asleep. Their absence wraps itself in the smoke or in the space between stairs, and a touch from a hand to a knee registers in the silence and brain as the slide of a mallet along the grooves of a gong. Bumping knees call to eyes that look away and suddenly wish for interruption, to be tucked back safely into any other night, reading a half-awake novel in a body-scented bed; the other person moving in and out closing up the various entrances to the house. Suddenly with one nudge of bare leg against leg, the danger of not living in a single obligation rushes out of the flesh in a frenzied take-off of mental flight. Until one of us visualizes pulling the elbow of the other for the effect of unbalancing our moral positions, toppling our lips onto each other, forging a necessity of hands and waists in the awkward, tipped-backward edge of passion. And one of us imagines pressing the other back across the damp wood of the porch to spread your gorgeous hair against an actual surface rather than the space between us. You smell like wine. And the next week we are still unable to stop touching accidentally at our places around the table, through the candles burning uselessly in too much electric light. The pleasure of cooking a large dinner for many people is that the ingredients fold into the recipe and the baking timer rings at the end. Never again will containers of flour, boxes of brown sugar, shakers of paprika be considered separately when we assimilate to the meal.

Workers (attendants)

Nights we lie beside her, our mouths
at her belly, counting

her breaths, the buzz, the gathering, long
done. We all began
inside her, like those lined up

inside her now, mere
idea of ourselves
unborn. We wash her body

ceaselessly, move our tongues
until all her hairs loosen. She

roams the brood, finds
another empty cell

& fills it. Morning comes &
she calms us, keeps us inside
until the dew burns off. This sodden

world. All winter

we huddled around her, kept her
warm. Those on the outside, those
farthest from her, died

first, their legs
gripped the others like a shawl.

Graham Foust

On the Evening of a Wedding

One day love
is mere
manipulation.

Someone needs something.

You sing them
your song.

On another day love
is purely
a possession.

You want something.

Someone paints
your picture.

You rock back and forth
between these days,
until a third day,
that day on which
the world
puts its mouth to yours.

The world's mouth is a church.

Your mouth, of course,
is a pictureless room
in which an afternoon's gods
get lost.

Peter Gizzi

It Was Raining in Delft

A cornerstone. Marble pilings. Curbstones and brick.
I saw rooftops. The sun after a rain shower.
Liz, there are children in clumsy jackets. Cobblestones
     and the sun now in a curbside pool.
I will call in an hour where you are sleeping. I've been walking
     for 7 hrs on yr name day.
Dead, I am calling you now.
There are colonnades. Yellow wrappers in the square.
Just what you'd suspect: a market with flowers and matrons,
     handbags.
Beauty walks this world. It ages everything.
I am far and I am an animal and I am just another I-am poem,
     a we-see poem, a they-love poem.
The green. All the different windows.
There is so much stone here. And grass. So beautiful each
     translucent electric blade.
And the noise. Cheers folding into traffic. These things.
     Things that have been already said many times:
leaf, zipper, sparrow, lintel, scarf, window shade.

Arielle Greenberg

Letters from Camp

Dear. It's like camp, our ivy union,
those buried dollars. It's like summer:
with each breeze, I get a box.
I'd better. It looks like I'm writing
you a letter. Love. Stop. Dear.
The artists are a brat. I slake
down a sandwich and run
for the mail. We sit around shop,
talk girl talk and all the girls agree—
in their slots, they'd prefer
mostly men, a bit of boy,
a pleading drunk. It's so hetero
around here. I am finding
new ways to touch the leather.
I prefer tape (can you hear
me?) and the newsprint
crushed inside, turning my skin
to type. You are my type
if only you'd grow back your hair.
Love. Stop. Dear. Here's
a postcard of my needs:
I want to see a wild animal
and tame it like a brute tongue.
I want to be fluent in the forest,
naked. I would like to release
the moths from their pulsing
quiver chest. Love. Stop.
P.S. I'm nothing like an arrow.
You would barely recognize me.
It's all the whites they change for us,
every Tuesday. Dear. Here's another request:
I would like you to send me the chain
made of lettered keys. We can spell

that word you mentioned. We can make it
quite an elegant fight. You'll be divine
if you send it priority. And a clock. Love.
Stop. Dear. I'd like a letter.
You sent a plastic fox to sit at my window;
a plastic lamb to by my bed. It made
us both laugh. I wear the ring
of watery compass so I won't get
lost again. But the woods, honey.
The what comes from trees.
They feel like poison willows.
I'm scared of the dark at night,
what it doesn't have lying in it,
its ominous rocks, so I walk back
in twos. I've made some friends.
Love. Stop. Dear. I am writing
home, saying save me from this whiskey
sour. My only sidecar should be you.

Saskia Hamilton

SPECIES OF AUDIBLES

Because I was to think otherwise. Because
we listened to the song in snatches, to
the symphony in small pieces, not to
follow, not to follow the next piece
or what was the following
song. The piece too long
for attention. Listening
akin to reading. I was
stranded on the voice.
He took my fingers
in his mouth. No, not
fingernails, not tongue,
not the temperature of the mouth, but the vibration,
always he was about to touch the throat,
the throat of the person speaking.

Matthea Harvey

In Defense of Our Overgrown Garden

Last night the apple trees shook and gave each lettuce a heart
Six hard red apples broke through the greenhouse glass and
Landed in the middle of those ever-so-slightly green leaves
That seem no mix of seeds and soil but of pastels and light and
Chalk x's mark our oaks that are supposed to be cut down
I've seen the neighbors frown when they look over the fence
And see our espalier pear trees bowing out of shape I did like that
They looked like candelabras against the wall but what's the sense
In swooning over pruning I said as much to Mrs. Jones and I swear
She threw her cane at me and walked off down the street without
It has always puzzled me that people coo over bonsai trees when
You can squint your eyes and shrink anything without much of
A struggle ensued with some starlings and the strawberry nets
So after untangling the two I took the nets off and watched birds
With red beaks fly by all morning at the window I reread your letter
About how the castles you flew over made crenellated shadows on
The water in the rainbarrel has overflowed and made a small swamp
I think the potatoes might turn out slightly damp don't worry
If there is no fog on the day you come home I will build a bonfire
So the smoke will make the cedars look the way you like them
To close I'm sorry there won't be any salad and I love you

Christian Hawkey

Fräulein, can you

                sometimes, when I can't sleep, I drag my sleeping bag
into the meadow's precise center
& crawl inside, head first. Fräulein, there is the stars'
ceaseless drilling. I close my eyes. Somewhere below me
a star-nosed mole cuts its webbed hand
on a shard of glass. I close my ears
& over my body the current of a young doe
eddies, ripples across the field, a low-lying midnight fog
swirling after her, falling back, suspended. I know you are close.
The scar across my cheek burns. I think of reentering
                your atmosphere,
                your long, burning hair

Don't move. The slightest motion

                & this landscape, erased by floodlights

CLARINET
for Yona

I am sometimes the clarinet
your parents bought
your first year in band,
my whole body alive
in your fingers, my one ear
warmed by the music
you breathe into it.
I hear your shy laugh
among the girls at practice.
I am not your small wrist
rising & falling as you turn
the sheet music,
but I want to be.
Or pinky bone, clavicle.
When you walk home
from school, birds call
to you in a language
only clarinets decipher.
The leaves whistle
and gawk as you pass.
Locked in my skinny box,
I want to be at least
one of the branches
leaning above you.

Steve Healey

INTERVIEW WITH A PIECE OF SMOKE

I can live if all the glass in this neighborhood
sleeps with me or lets me sleepwalk
through the don't-walk paradigm.
Red quickens here and eats the white lines
or throws me from window to window.
My fingers unmarry their prints,
and listen, the poly-cotton whispers
pass on Avenue A. On the curb
tired crutches not going anywhere
once had the urge to fit more in the frame,
and because the air is a little medieval today,
flecked with silver codes, it can bend
and bend like cellophane to include
that far castle with the human
but cloud-size head peering out
to give the effect of nearness. In fact,
everything rests on the tip of a unicorn's horn.
It casts a mile-long shadow: listen,
the tender thunder. It's almost too quiet,
that fear of being damaged, it's like
you telling me how a blister feels on your hand
surrounded by maybe 15,000 nerve ends
asking to be rubbed. It's like I'm fluid
slipping away, I'm an earthling
and a mint farmer saying goodbye
to my rain-soaked rows, I don't know
how anyone keeps breathing while addicted
to that sudden harvest, but it makes me
want to be born again with a caul
over my face. I could be premonition city
with a boy loping through my streets
or a boy going down on the man he'll become—
either way, it's motility the windows want,

and the faster you say it, the faster
I buff my boots with a horsehair brush,
the sooner a horse comes and takes me away,
a white horse with you on it and a horn
jutting from its forehead, the sooner
we come to a piece of music and see
that last night is there wearing
black lipstick, or the lipstick
wears your lips, and we are alive.

Brian Henry

Look Around

Sometimes I wonder about the power of invention.
If a look can replace the vigor I'm missing.
The woman I'm watching does not notice me.
Monday she brings petals with their stalks to her window.
Friday she removes them dried from the sill.
Her weekends are spent flowerless yet apart.
This is her summer habit and one I've come to own,
if not to love, for the habits I love are my own.
One manner of heartbreak is more abstract
than one manner of lust; this inequality
will expand to embrace what it will.
I once thought she smiled at me as I typed.
I returned the smile into the darkness
but I refuse to say *the darkness smiled back.*
The darkness was not even that dark.
The light from my computer screen at times
distracts me from my windowside vigil.
The window is a marshal of sainthood.
The window knows its job, and does it.
I have no job but to watch, and this I do
daily, and with the joy resignation brings.
Sometimes I wonder about the loss this entails.
Sometimes I wonder if my vision opens
only for windows, how I will navigate my life
in a cell. If a harbinger of spring is really desire
or only the private awareness of what
the woman I'm watching decides is her hell.
I have seen no demons in her apartment.
No demons have entered or left during my vigil.
But a demon arriving before I began
could be there still, awander in the rooms
and wanting to ask about the flowers but afraid
to ask would risk a warmth. Across the street
my apartment is cold despite the air.
Her flowers would not survive here.
But then, they will not survive anywhere.

Christine Hume

ANIMAL HOUSE SHAPE OF GOD

We stood beside the unreal.
It seemed withdrawn: a meandering line
in the dog-smelling wind.

We tracked every acre in full fury:
the intense white of violet
light out of its tree.

Eyeless black wolves lope like
lapping fur currents.
Their thousand syncopations brighten

a splitting silence; smoke
runs down ridges.
Everyone else's son is in jail.

Why should our thoughts slope
below us? Grazing grotesques of rock—
see what's diamondback-struck.

We change body temperature.
We are a noise, depending. The mind
blanks out a fault, shoots into river.

When one circles another,
it teaches forty-one examples.
How many wolves we did not know.

We calm our hands by holding sticks.
Calling your name
rips open the sky's gut: branches

and sharp stars pulse until calling out
bleeds your name please
make it drain all shape from our heart:

Henry Israeli

SWAY
for JG

The lassitude of a summer's day wrapped in the sadness
of a winter's day, an elevator transporting a pinecone

from the basement to the penthouse, as if tragedy
were something one hummed aloud, lackadaisically.

In the garden, the tulips, far flung and red, muffle cries
and spread their legs. Morning rain whispers another tribe's

perfume, swept up by a broom miles away.
There's a pond where newborns, rising like lilies

to the surface, inhale and dive back to the floor,
playing make-believe in a weightless world. . . .

But your sway is lighter still than all their buoyant gestures:
it trickles away. Remember an autumn, years ago, when a nail

shot perfectly through a window without shattering the glass,
so light was the touch of the hand that hammered it there.

Major Jackson

URBAN RENEWAL XII.

North of Diamond Lake, the Cascades, crossmarks
of yew trees, calligraphic leafblades like credits,—
scrolling, behind the scenes, relegated,
we're lost and drive to a pass snow-blocked.
Listening to THIS AMERICAN LIFE,
the brute scoop broadcast as matter-of-fact,
our lives armed with tears in four acts:
Bonding's like scaling Kilimanjaro. Quite
naturally, love's whacked our ribs to steel,—
so, we're better off shoveling vignettes?
Imagine Auden dear penning antisonnets,
reasoning we've relinquished a good deal
of vocation. A frayed-winged hawk squawks
above in piercing kilowatts and anoints these summits
coolly with his feathered-blood. What's lost?
the kickback of Orpheus; his acoustics lack
confession, and still we turn and inch downhill
in narrow S's, guided by the compass
below his heart. Suffering in nature, the valley rising
on the backs of roadkill. Darling, how else
do we know we are here? These leaves
pinwheeling are songs I sing both grievous
and bracing; each groan puts us closer to the grave.

Lisa Jarnot

THEY LOVED THESE THINGS TOO

The sun the moon the stars the polar ice caps and the ice cream cones the city streets the side streets and the small TV the curve of flesh around the food the road maps and November and the tiny birds and also certain people and they loved the special chairs and also stuffed things and the carnival and big rings and the o rings and they loved the oranges in bags and Florida and Texas and the hotel room and they loved the chili on the highway that they loved as if they loved the onramp and the way that people called and the natural forces of destruction and the sea they loved the sea and also boats and sailing ships and whales they loved and sea birds in varieties and then they loved the choice of drinks to drink and also beer they loved the times that others liked them that they loved and also they loved things all shaped like tigers and they loved the zoo.

Devin Johnston

PYRAMUS & THISBE

When there is love
'between us,' I think of

a curtain wall:
hair-line cracks transport all

our talk to us,
and map the faults of commerce;

or a border collie,
emissary

of milk-white teeth beneath
black dew-flaps,

who occupies the quilt—
an ampersand in sleep.

You press your lips
to stone—a wall we've built.

W. B. Keckler

A WEDDING

Did you know in China
they marry the unlucky dead?

Two strangers who died young,
their families meet
to exchange photographs,
trinkets.

Nothing gruesome, no actual
use of corpses,
although the couple's ashes
might be mixed.

Their parents feel a little better then.
All the years they spent raising them . . .

Life is what the living *take;*
we refuse to be occupied by the dead.

The dead are there merely to prop us up.

When they understand this at last,
they will be happy,

they will find heaven.

Joanna Klink

Apology

Lately, too much disturbed, you stay breathing in me
and I believe you. How could I not feel
you were misspent, there by books stacked clean on glass,
or outside the snow arriving as I am still arriving.
If the explanations amount to something, I will tell you.
It is enough, you say, that surfaces grow so distant.
Maybe you darken, already too much changed,
maybe in your house you would be content where
no incident emerges, but for smoke or glass or air,
such things held simply to be voiceless.
And if you mean me, I believe you.
Or if you should darken, this inwardness would be misspent,
and wincing I might pause, and add to these meager
incidents the words. Some books
should stay formal on the shelves.
So surely I heard you, in your complication aware,
snow holding where it might weightless rest,
and should you fold into me—trackless, misspent,
too much arranged—I might believe you
but swiftly shut, lines of smoke rising through snow,
here where it seems no good word emerges.
Though it is cold, I am aware such reluctance
could lose these blinking hours to simple safety.
Here is an inwardless purpose.
In these hours when snow shuts, it may be we empty,
amounting to something. How could I not
wait for those few words, which we might enter.

Noelle Kocot

Bicycle Poem

There were cathedrals falling out of your eyes
And your arms were the handlebars
I held in an abbreviated dream of crushed petals
Strewn across the limpid avenues.

I said, "I have poems for you"
But my words were lost in the wind.
I said, "I love you"
And you drifted into sleep.

And so I said nothing and rode you in and out of the rooms
Where we had stretched the boundaries of the soul
Like and endless sheet
And I felt you waking up between my legs.

Aaron Kunin

THE SORE THROAT

The throat is
sore for a
word. It is
sore with word-

desire, desire
for the word "she."
The word "she": will
it appear? Will

she appear?
(Is the word
"she" a she?)
She is a

word I always,
without knowing,
had in my mind.
Once, to my shame,

I had no
idea
what to do
with the word

"she"; now it seems
like I don't know
any other
word. It seems like

everything
is a she,
money is
a she (you're

so complete you
don't have to think
about money!
You have so much

money you
don't know what
knowing is!),
knowing is

a she, and in
heaven, god is
a she. No more
Herr Gott, from now

on, no more
seigneur, no
more boy-god:
the end! But

won't she start to
wonder: "If there's
no word for 'he,'
if everything

is a she,
why would we
have to have
a word for

it? If this word
appears every-
where, it won't mean
anything." And

at last she
may say to
you: "You are
my own good

boy. For me
there's no choice:
no other
boy will do."

Christian Langworthy

Why I Look at Girls

I look at girls as an act of escapism
While reading books at Barnes & Noble
On the death of poetry. I look at girls
Because I think Darryl Hannah was perfect
In the role of a cavewoman.
I look at girls especially when I have my beer
Goggles on. I look at girls for ideological reasons
I have yet to ponder. I look at girls
When Baywatch isn't on.
I look at girls left exposed by the fall
Of the "Iron Curtain" & I look
Jealously at the half a billion comrades
Lusting after Chairman Mao behind the Great China Wall,
But most of all, I look at girls as I am an agent
For the CIA. I look at girls who check out other men.
I look at girls who lust after girls. I look at girls though
Sometimes I am frightened to death
Taking my goggles off. I look at girls
For intellectual reasons, correlating Marxism,
Gender, & Colonialism from Mary Wollstonecraft
To Jamaica Kincaid. I look at girls despite
The fact that Molly Ringwald can't act. I look
At girls based on the recommendation of my therapist
Who says I need to break out of my shyness
Maybe next year. I look at girls ever since I dated
An American Gladiator known in the business as "Ice"
Who likes to beat people up. I look at girls
To get back at City Hall for closing down
PeepWorld. I look at girls who return my glance
Because I am a sensitive, considerate man.
I look at girls only when I run
For President. I look at girls in Hollywood

Even if they're on Heidi Fleiss's payroll.
I look at girls who study the paintings of
Van Gogh, Bonnard, Matisse,
And some other famous guys I can only remember
With the help of a Metropolitan Museum of Modern Art
Brochure. I look at girls who read Rousseau,
Locke, and Rawls, and then again, I look at girls who
Aren't cross-eyed after reading Rawls, Locke,
& Rousseau. I look at girls when no one
Else looks at them because I am a sensitive, considerate
Man. I look at girls who aren't really girls,
But never for more than a second
& never twice. I look at girls on film.
I look at girls who grow older.

Tanya Larkin

CHO-FU-SA

It is what the river-merchant's wife writes her water-bound husband.
Cho-Fu-Sa being how far, exactly? And will I ever know the truth

that is the distance one can travel away from the self to another
without breaking apart, until I have arrived, myself, white-hot

and thirsty, looking to tie one on in a three-syllable town:
the lover, the beloved, and the invisible animal they've raised

between them, into the wilderness between them of horns and roots,
blank sheets of paper mottled with light that sifts down through

leaf-cover, underbush. How will I know this port town is the right
town until I stand at its wall, ripened by the miles I've walked

and sometimes sprinted with tears scattered down, like now, because
no matter how you reassure us, you will never come back to us

the same, but always wearing the other like a burning we must
reach through, the bright, new fever of home. Never mind that love

contracts the world, that if you bind your breath together, we are only
one breath away. Let us in. We have fistfuls of sand, foreign coins,

and gold string, blossoms and wishes, buttons that fell from your cuff.
Those days you were tenaciously single and uncertain, or

ecstatic with resolve, to hold out for the one, the town of two-in-one.
Where the swell rushes the shore nonchalantly, striking like a vow

until there's no more sand to strike upon. Let us in to lob our small
gifts above your path. The arms to fly out with generous abandon.

The hand to open. The hand to open. The hands opening as you pass.
If you should look back to find us scrambling behind you, sweeping

the floor for grain or confetti caught and freed by your veil,
who can blame us? No—embrace us, lock us into your town.

We won't be here much longer. Because this is the part when
you want to be alone, when you feed us to the tigers and kiss.

Katy Lederer

IN LAS VEGAS

1.
When I write a novel in Vegas, I ask myself what other people will think.
When I write a novel, I think a lot about eating.
When I call my friend, he gets very excited.
Out of my window I see a huge mountain.
Its striations make it look as if the rain has fallen sideways on it. Over
          the years
I have danced a lot. I have thought to become a novelist.
I see a mountain that looks as if drenched by the rain. I see a sky
Wherein clouds drift by slowly and unendingly.
Pistons go up and down. Pendulums swing back and forth.
If a person who is in love with me reads this, they will care.
If someone who hates me reads it, they will dismiss me as an impostor.

2.
Trees are like cairns. The yard is clean. The door is opened
to let in air. I have driven great distances and listened to a lot of music.
I read things that make me jealous. Alone.
I read about people I know. All women want to be beautiful.

3.
The pool's light like moonlight.
The idea is to exercise caution and not give it up to them.
To say love and not be determined to show it then makes one a bastard.
To make proclamations as these are very pretty things to make
and to script them out and cause ugly havoc in the universe
we then must know. Over the hills there are lights.
Over the hills there are lights and this heat.
You have been the measure of all greatness.
It is pleasant of you in my mind to have been so.
You please god to love then if measuring greatness within me
found succubus to be fled, sent out, and adored.
Pray for me, I be less wholesome when trees sway.
Winds. Winds go these everywhich way.

4.
I like the sky. And I do not do
the opposite of what the trees do.
Interesting. I love you
is like sitting on a bench and you don't
mean it when you say it.
Someone else has made you say it.

Lisa Lubasch

Enough To Say

> . . . but there was the larger pattern
of the fall to keep in mind. A saddish contempt for
getting things wrong.
The tritones kept us happy, or enamored
with the prospect of new pain, another
resolve. All through the broken lines,
you went to my heart . . .

> The saying we knew
to fall from (the way everything fell
when it was time)—were we the only ones it didn't notice, account for, take
into account? I love you in a language we've agreed to keep
quiet about. In a diligent refusal of what's ours.

Sarah Manguso

THE PIANO

I try to imagine the lid closing but it won't.
The keys shine at me in black and white.
They are evil. I am evil. My dream is evil.
I whisper the word *concupiscence* into the open lid,
Which is a sin. I am so full I cannot breathe.
The stars arc overhead. I am in a field.
The piano has followed me here—softly, softly.
It spits music at me, then blankets me in music.
I put it on a leash as an experiment.
It whimpers, then is still. No music comes.
I fall in love with my pet.
We walk through the field.
The piano spells my name in keys.
It plays me a piece I have never heard
Rolling gently behind me—it begins
with the sound of light moving
and ends with the sound of a sun going out.
They are the same even though the picture changes.
I make love to my piano in the open field.
I have nothing to do with the universe.
I prefer to stay here with you.

Body Cavity

You have the right to remain silent.

A videotape recording of this procedure shall be made.

Videotaping shall begin as soon as my search begins. I shall first state the date and time, clearly, and the camera operator shall then enter this information electronically onto the videotape.

The camera operator during your strip search shall be of the same sex you are, unless you request otherwise. This option may not be possible in some areas.

During this search, assuming compliancy, a privacy barrier (e.g. curtain, wall, sheet, screen, door, cardboard, beach towel, piece of wood, office cubicle divider or any other similar barrier preventing visual inspection of the private parts) shall be placed between you and the camera operator. If compliancy is not assured and/or there is the threat of your physical resistance, camera operators are instructed to videotape both you and the officer conducting the search simultaneously to protect against allegations of improper physical interactions, in which case all or partial nudity may be captured on videotape.

The purpose of this search will be stated just before it is to begin. There is some evidence that needs to be obtained. While conducting the search of your body, I shall, when possible, wear gloves. If it is not possible to wear gloves, I shall wash my hands thoroughly before returning to work. Then I shall wash them again.

You will be asked to hand over any hazardous materials before the search begins. Failure to do so could result in hazardous conditions for you and for me.

You will shake your hair vigorously. You will lean forward slightly against a stable countertop or the hood of an official vehicle. I will stand slightly to one side of your body. I will begin to search your hair and your head. I will run my fingers through your hair. If you prefer to run your own fingers through your hair, that's okay too, and I will watch this.

Next, I will inspect your nasal, ear and mouth cavities, including the crevice behind your ear. You will lift your hair up off your neck. If you have any false teeth, you will need to remove them now.

You will stand with your arms extended, fingers spread. I will unfold your collar, cuffs, sleeves and any other creases found in your clothing. I will squeeze your collar. I will run my hands over your shoulder and down the length of your arms, down to your hands, then back up and into your armpits. I will unbutton your shirt and pay special attention to your armpits, the small of your back, your chest.

You will be taken to a more private area, where you will be asked to remove your bra and lean forward. I will take hold of the center of your bra and shake it. I will instruct you to lift your breasts so that I may inspect under them.

I will descend to your waistband. I will run my hands over it and squeeze it. I will unbuckle you, unbutton you. I will run my hands along your waist and proceed then to the buttocks and legs. Your legs will be slightly apart. I will unzip your pants or skirt. I will be using both hands at this juncture. I will be paying special attention to the seams. As I check each leg, I will check the crotch area. I will run my hand well up into the groin.

I will instruct you to squat down and cough. This will permit me a visual check of your darker areas.

Where possible, I will use tongs or forceps to assist me in difficult to reach areas.

Then I will switch to the other side of your body, conditions permitting, and repeat the procedure from step one, methodically and with great care, this time more familiar with the curvature of your body, the nature of its hiding places.

I will proceed as quickly as I'm comfortable, and with sensitivity to the subtle responses I provoke in you. What items I find during the search will be placed in my plastic evidence bag.

We shall begin the search now. The time is midnight.

Cate Marvin

ALBA: ABERDEEN

A sky that blue is not a sad thing.
Some nights are not worth sleeping. And knowing
we'll never see a blue like that

ever again is fine. There are
nights not worthy of sleep. When the blue brims
like that and swallows the town

in its huge tear, the little
bridges we walk back over leave us. We're almost
back at your house, so we sit

in the alley and wait a while
for the sky to become normal. Our mouths marry
in smoke and the aftertaste

of Scotch. A man walks by
with his dog. Gulls shriek and dive; their noises
are terrible; the town wakes.

We pace some more before
returning each other's hands, then decide to sleep
the day. Your wife is waking

for work. We are almost
asleep, in our separate rooms. Our lungs are blue
from breathing that color.

Our faces wear the same
expression. The sky is incapable of anything bluer.
Our hearts cannot be redder.

Anthony McCann

Confessions

beginnings

Before money and California;
before the state of Massachusetts
there was a river and it had a name.
Another mossy indian-sounding name.
Woodlands Indian.
There was a river and it loved the land.
The land was rich with whatever land
is rich with, minerals and vitamins I guess.
But then it was scraped away, into the river,
with imported tools, by incompetent invaders
who were cruel and stupid
and filled the land with package stores
and the towns grew and grew around them.
And into this land I was born.
Or so it is said. All I want to tell here Lord
is that I do not know where I really came from
when I was born into this life.
But I was content to suck.
And so I grew to the next stage.

adolescence

I could call this a revolt.
This next stage.
I don't remember
when it started.
I could call it Woburn.
Or I could call it Braintree.
What I remember is that boredom,
its shape. I have driven
that car. But this one time
I was in love—this was before California.

This was after Panama
but before the Gulf.
I had a brand new pair
of excellent boots and
I drove my car fast
along the river's curves.
Forgive me Lord, I didn't know
what I was really like.

confession

There was a young woman from another state who in my youth I
mistreated. We said angry and sappy and stupid things as youths
will do because we thought we understood our tongue. There are no
photographs of us. But take it that she was an unattractive girl and I was
an unattractive boy. Together we did unattractive things. Until then I
had imagined that I was kind; a somehow wounded young man. I don't
remember what actors I admired. But then I discovered arrogance and
cruelty and silence in particular and she went back to her boyfriend a
small and truly kind boy who played the acoustic guitar. I went and
stood at the edge of a frozen parking lot on the edge of that city where
the city gives way and the liquor gives way to an empty Taco Time and
the death of all enthusiasm. I had some other friends with me, they were
asleep in the car and, Lord, I thought they all looked retarded.

received wisdom

Once there was a boy
who wouldn't look up
or he wouldn't look down
I can't remember
and in his mouth he held
a precious stone
He was a stupid boy
The End
Or once there was a boy
who lived all alone in the world

except for his friend
Mr. Egg
And he got what he deserved

and the next stage

And the next stage
is California.

california

The coast was covered in fog
as I came up over
the ridge in our car
listening to a sad
and triumphant
California song.
I was some kind
of superstar, pissing
in the parking lot
over the Pacific
near the RVs.
What else
can I say?
I came here
searching for you,
through the
interior, dry like a mouth.
Subsisting on bagels
and dope.
And I drove on
into the city, where I went amongst them.
I examined their flesh
and found it to be weak.
Pushed to a certain wall,
my arms and legs
bent to their pleasure,
I expired at dawn.
Giving up the ghost, this body and breath, up
into the cruel blue air.
Beginning again, naked and curled
in a stranger's bed.

Aaron McCollough

Eros, Ethos, Economuos

The air is good in here
we say of the pine-tree

and breaking twigs to move
the soul with what we have

to stick against the fact
of empty sky.

Just look! Cardinals
have nested here since fall

as we have come to rest
and raise our young

in a dangerous
and tangible wilderness.

Secrets inside we can't
quite name. Hopes. Shapely wants.

The silhouette of cones,
which don't resemble cones

in silhouette but tress
upended. Dear, we lease

the stem alive and smooth,
though tearing the bark off—

the wet, green, denuded
careen of this not ours

to love.

Jeffrey McDaniel

Hunting for Cherubs

If you heard your lover scream in the next room, and you ran in and saw his pinkie on the floor in a small puddle of blood, you wouldn't rush to the pinkie and say *Darling, are you okay?* No, you'd wrap your arms around his shoulders and worry about the pinkie later. The same holds true if you heard the scream, ran in, and saw his hand, or, God forbid, his whole arm. But suppose you hear your lover scream in the next room, and you run in, and his head is on the floor, next to his body, which do you rush to and comfort first?

Mark McMorris

FROM THE BLAZE OF THE POUI

Tell me again, Love, what is a wedding?

A wedding is earth and water
and a species of irreducible light
and the flat belly of a harbor
and a mango about to ripen and fall into gravity's caress
and the waves subsiding
              and resuming their concerto in a minor key
and the rush hour canceled by the stun of auspicious beginnings
      with even the bride asleep, in that hour
          when the songbirds begin to light up the harbor
      and the groom sleepwalks to the pot of heliconia,
         thinking that the day is not yet begun
    with the shoes lonely
            and the corsage unlinked and the perfumes
      innocently waiting, omens of infinity
and the day of a wedding is a perfect kiss
      ten thousand kisses like fireflies on a rampage
      ten thousand kisses like long grass swaying in sun
and the words have come to us that we like
and are content to be here, named and not named aloud,
the word *abide,* and *confide,* and others
the words—ugly but useful—*social cement,* and others
and void has no seat among
the words *gift* and *Eros,* and the words
convivial amity, and others

A wedding—this wedding—is the perfect resolution
the globe of festivals, with the intention
of a meeting that began in another decade
and will continue later this evening with the dance
and on into the enchained days it will go on
and so into folded dark

and at a wedding, the guests will see
know the conduct of infinity, although
it stay only in desire, and the geometry
of unbounded happiness is finally felt to
be the case: the circle of the wedding
hangs in space like a time without borders

Richard Meier

ECLIPSED

Let me propose to you this way.
From here to Canada, where the tundra
Offers the sky like bare flesh beside its bleakness,
During the latest eclipse
Retinas were burned, lines were crossed
That seemed like opposites until they bent space,
As touching you more and more suddenly wasn't,
Where the occluded sun, eyeball, and occluding moon
All take a role. Aw, one guy was stuck
Behind a milk truck in traffic. The stainless steel
Was protecting the milk, see.
The damage came undone like a ravel of hair
Which didn't belong to anyone.
Logic is furious.
Run a little faster, dame, demimonde.
I'll try to keep up
While my eyes ache in sympathy
With the dim shapes we used to call the world.
I can't say I'm sorry,
You who are to me both sun and moon.

Lynn Melnick

Manhattan Valley

Who am I if not outside, a blizzard and borrowed
but hardly noticed, a drizzle. Let's look at this objectively.
I am always cold. Every step is streetwater, spell

surrounds the building. It must be noticed, to wail out
sirens grandly, to scarlet a sky this stern and dreary,
from black to black to plum. Lightning has let me live

one more storm. It's embarrassing, for God's sake, how I stay.
Here in our hollow, the gourds grow impossibly up,
waiting for a comeback. Tell me what this downcast means

and I will tell you where I've run from, a street
with strains of summer, a room that cannot hold us in its grave
drapery. I know you so well here; I keep always in

the same arrangement, lolling extravagant, sinful, buried
in possession. This is lucky and lucky isn't what it used to be,
for either of us. Most times I am too unbraced to bear it,

quite soprano and flung. Where is the hand at my waist,
and the dancing? Not some tricked-out voodoo,
but what's all around me. I miss you, you can't even imagine.

Sometimes I bite to bleeding; I need things on a grander scale.
There are rules, which mean it can't be this cozy
forever. Hat on the bed, shoes on the table. We are doomed.

THE SKULL RING

I am very excited about the skull ring. I didn't know anyone would think I wanted a silver skull ring. Now, when I am rude to those who oppose me, I can just look down at the skull ring. It has ruby chips in the eyes! Ruby chips like the nasty flame in my own eyes when I am insulted or reviled. No one will dare oppose me now in my hometown. For a very long time I have avoided rings because none of them seemed right for me. A skull ring is actually a good complement to my diabolical will. Thank you very much for the skull ring.

Ange Mlinko

Just Dump Me on the Palace Steps

As a source of information to the biologist I put my loves in the running
like a stripe in the cake:

We stuff garbage under the porch, two girls laughing through a
balalaika spy a rotweiler, one asks me to cross the street with
her, they'll tell you they like your shoes.

The weather drops like a chateau on a television the avant-garde crocus
on us, window's open to the last thing I looked at, no wonder it's so
freaking cold it's like the dictionary!

I'm not always proud to be a bored clerk, burning origami, I was in the
office of this matchmaker, advice columnist. Her fur coat was
stretched upon the divan no client's invited to sit on, I was privy to
her practice, took the Myers-Briggs, beat it out of there.

This is what will happen: oxidation & reduction, hair like a complete
shakespeare raked open, rags to riches on which is written: I don't
like it when you watch television in the frozen room I'm outside of in
cybernetic frenzy of feedback relationship (crime & punishment).

A doodad to put the eye to & shatter the world! All kinds of light
become my job to shepherd. As the record draws the needle in, the
eye of your beloved is represented by a diamond.

The thief dawns on love, so let him have the jewel to guarantee your
eyes, given to you for nothing & held in common with everyone.

Jennifer Moxley

From A Distance I Can See

You have a lovely and familiar gravity,
and like in the apartment of my youthful reveries
each time I walk into you my city-bound Greyhound
rolls through the rain drenched streets,
a lightscape full of traffic and wondrous people
lies ahead, once you've caught view they shall demand
the tapering of all your beautiful fingers,
they shall tell your eyes to stop shooting such glances
for they are blocking your lips from seeming
red as they are, and what of gentle memory,
it frames your face and returns home devastated
to inform me of such boundaries shifting
that in them, as in you, my dreams shall rest just dreams,
the rain drenched city of adulthood, vanish in advances.

Maggie Nelson

SUBWAY IN MARCH, 5:45 P.M.

I take the long way home, knowing
I am free to choose happiness

or wander off into the tunnel
On the platform two teenagers french kiss, her lips

are enormous and soft and he seems at home with them
I feel crumpled like the pastel houses lining the canal

I am transporting an adorable succulent
the size of an infant's fist, holding it close as if

it were the one thing I had to keep alive
and thinking how much easier it would be

if all I had to love were this small plant
and then I wouldn't be so hard on you

and we could like the world before distrusting it
Stop performing ourselves and let the pith of us

hang out. All these permutations of esteem and ridicule
when all I want is to stay focused on everyday life

What other kind of life is there?
All the world knows it, it's a miracle

The blue womb of evening
The nimble sparrow, the smug duck in the pond

The eruption of flowering quince
O shackle us to the rock of it

we will try to love each other
though there's wind on our heads

and we cannot read minds
The train jumps above ground

and stripes the car in gold light
It's the light of early spring

Daniel Nester

THIRD MAISIE POEM

I try not to get fancy or fussy
when I speak of you. I fear
commonplace things, common
words, and so much about you
is so basic that I'm left with no
distinguishing marks to speak of.
My tangent is this—this morning,
daydreaming in my solitary bed,
I listened to yet another narrative
country song. It addressed the plight
of a man and a woman, of course,
but what was different was the voice,
that it was the woman who gave
the details of the certain tragedy.
The man jack-knifed his truck
on the road, leaving the baby
and mother at home. So as the sun
came up, I had the urge
to address you, to adorn
your relentless miracles,
to reimagine a whole lexicon
for you. It was as simple as that.

Hoa Nguyen

[CALMLY GRASS BECOMES A WAVE]

Calmly grass becomes a wave
See the body parts you name
unsoothes you where you slip
trying to write or wake up

The songs overlap each other   baby

an echo knell a creased pit
an animal
an animal

Hello   call me

Travis Nichols

Wild is the Wind

There is a movie called "She's Gotta Have It."
There is a blizzard in Massachusetts today.
Twenty-one people died in Chicago last night.
Two of my friends live there,
but I have never wanted to live there
because it is cold there and people die
from the cold and the wind and from each other.
There is a movie called "Chicago."
I saw it yesterday in Massachusetts.
The wind is shaking our house this morning
but it's warm inside. One of my friends
in Chicago loves to have sex, the other
thinks she might but she's scared
because she passed out the first time
she had sex with someone else but that
was only a few months ago before it got so cold
in Chicago. I've had sex with one of my friends from Chicago
but not the other one though I wouldn't have sex
with either of them now after I've read how it is always
colder in Chicago than it is in Massachusetts
because of the wind. "Wild is the Wind" is a song
by Nina Simone about not having sex with your friends
in Chicago. That's not true. Twenty-one people
died in Chicago last night but not two of my friends
or me because I live in Massachusetts.

Geoffrey Nutter

II:II

Look—the moon is a perfect circle.
A circle itself is perfect.
Please don't go behind the buildings yet again.
I have watched you all evening.
I have compared my life to yours and found mine lacking.
You are leaving me.
And you will never even know what it was.
To see a sliver of your brilliance as you finally disappeared.
I have touched the part of you that never felt me.
I have touched you all the way to untouchability.

G. E. Patterson

The Saint's First Wife Said

I woke to your face not looking at me
but at the bird that settled on your wrist,
lured by food. Its trust, for once, was rewarded.
You offered the bird everything you had.

I remember. That is how it began
with us: You held out your hand; I took it.

Ethan Paquin

Woe

No God's rain petals—

      puddled, shallow
dreams and drifts

as airy as lambs' eyes

A breeze tosses
      light sentencery

for God loves me

and hid me next to you

D. A. Powell

[FIRST FUGUE]

sweet birds sang: *there is trouble in paradise today.*   and we sweated each other away: shirtless
you and I afforded ourselves: a land traversed many times.   nights of undoing
lover divine and perfect comrade.   *I always wanted someone like you.*   now the ground is braking

visitation is brief but exact.   smiles grow a little sharper.   no more expectations
ears in lips and no more wit.   *and I'm still real hot then you kiss me there.*   we toy in earnest
slow tyranny of moonlight: dead boys make the sweetest lovers.   if they could all be   finale

they pass too quickly out of breath.   *I feel real when you touch me.*   the night is an open "o"
erased metropolis reassembled: the anatomy remembers where it came from.   up as if from subways
reveries are rivers: *why don't you take me to heaven?*   the shiny buckle unfastens   at last

Kevin Prufer

Ars Poetica

I've written love notes all my life—
the letter I dropped from the window, stained and yellow;

the one curled into the beggar's cup.
The empire fell around me

like snow, so the citizens cringed in the streets,
their laces untied—blank-faced and strange.

I've written love notes and I do not know
to whom. In all directions, creased between bricks

or dropped from my fingers into gutters
so someone might find them and smile. Useless notes,

empty and vaguely
sad. I did nothing to help

while the empire limped into the park like a wounded car,
but composed while the crying shuddered

to a close and the buses stalled in the alleys.
Once, a group of hungry girls knotted on the street corner

called my name. Their hair was white
with snow, their lashes wet.

Love notes leaked from my hand as I walked past.
I have always been a gorgeous mind, light-in-the-eye

and dreaming. Always a work of art, a perfection
of limbs and hair, an arc in the marble

of my writing arm. Down and down my letters fell
while the empire closed.

Heather Ramsdell

Moveable Figures

rather deception than retreat, painted in flesh, in broken arcade, dust and
flecks of red remain

in the instance you and me, by small degrees able aberrations in flesh,
part hiding part enjoying being swallowed

we are very much particles flung here which stuck, are in accordance
with a theory of relations, never in this picture completely enough

from the scientist's window in *Rappaccini's Daughter,* facing a garden of
unnamed flowers, insects in poison, wounds for a mouth in
speaking from my heart we are made

today and tomorrow, forever will always be there

your hand or never, look or never, now or how

your hair moved, the stars by small degrees did, let us leave this spot

not exactly putting your finger there, in flesh, first wet then dry, first yes
amid rubble, first involuntary thirst

had shifted, this is not your fault—will I see you again? could we meet
would you like to go, like to the movies, or where you live?

in the instance of yes amid rubble, would you want me always "there"?
would you partway, in probable future a not undesirable wish

twirling, helpless, insects from the scientist's house, in the theater of
response, I brought you a flower

forever would always be there, what is your complaint—time was very
   difficult tonight for tonight we are the real, to wait to stop to say to
   kiss to sleep

to have to point to want to go to have, flowers for a flower, this instant

this instant, being foolish, you have broken, this is a bitter ending, I hate
   indiscretions, I have to crush you, my heart

half nude, the other half dramatic ruin of the nude, like in true love to
   shreds by piece by night unspooling the days events deep threads catch

here is the plane of the table the meat, and now a finger put in the abyss

if at all possible, the "I" in "to miss" by small degrees able to conceive of
   leaving the theater, eventually offering beloved eventually

Claudia Rankine

FROM Testimonial

As if I craved error, as if love were ahistorical,
I came to live in a country not at first my own
and here came to love a man not stopped by reticence.

And because it seemed right
that love of this man would look like freedom,

the lone expanse of his back
would be found land, I turned,

as a brown field turns, suddenly grown green,
for this was the marriage waited for: the man
desiring as I, movement toward mindful and yet.

It was June, brilliant. The sun higher than God.

Hotel Lullaby

No matter how often you knock
on the ocean the ocean

just waves. No matter
how often you enter the ocean

the ocean still says
no one's home. You must leave

her dear Ursula. As I write this
they polish the big

chandelier. Every prism
a sunset in abstract

or bijou foyer depending
on where you stand.

They take it apart every Fall
& call it Spring cleaning.

They bring me my tea.
They ask me my name

& I tell them—Ursula,
I don't even know

how to miss who you left.

Pam Rehm

Vow II

Willing to give thy Essence
I confess, thy face
Is my holy joy
I picture a fountain
How shall I embrace it
The mountain of breathing-time

Thou art to me a phantom
Affecting my heart, I swoon
Because I am flesh
To be near thine own bosom
What other life is there
I place all things in echo
from you, I do call on you,
Fall on my face
I must confess, I do

Peter Richards

AWAY FROM YOU THE SEAFLOOR'S LONGITUDINAL

Away from you the seafloor's longitudinal
grasses pump their anxiety and New World
pretenses up past a thicket of foam where every
day the same gull sits taped to rock smoking
a Newport and waiting for his brother to deliver
the revised figures, the linoleum swatches.
Away from you the breezeway's hand-me-down
camisole sits attentively unfolding the stairs
where I saw you descend into the source of all waters,
a minnow of sunscreen alive in your hand.
What witness discourages my brain from unfolding
another gushing hyacinth whose tan lines lead
to a room already slandered, already recurring,
for the wall here are lathered with flowers,
flowers from the forties, absolutely hyacinths
repeating their death-gasp up past the ceiling
where some truly old money sits squirreled away
from one day installing a fan. If I were to shave you
and not avoid life. If I could just lie there beneath
you like a tidal pool utterly hopeless and open,
it would be as if I push upon a tube of cadmium,
the toxicity warning just now tarnishing off,
just now insinuated into the work, the lungs,
the blood, it's the blood where a word could not
keep itself still and falls away from the foil
and onto this paper I send along with a little
salt to the shiny red apex of you.

Elizabeth Robinson

Snow

The purpose of the blanket
is not to cover but to fall.

You were made to
recognize, but poorly,

your lover.   A puppet

crudely carved in your likeness

beseeches your help.
Thus your fine seam
suspends the curtain

and your reflection bleaches
its own fabric whose referral
is late and harassed.

Matthew Rohrer

CREDO

I believe there is something else

entirely going on but no single
person can ever know it,
so we fall in love.

It could also be true that what we use
everyday to open cans was something
much nobler, that we'll never recognize.

I believe the woman sleeping beside me
doesn't care about what's going on
outside, and her body is warm
with trust
which is a great beginning.

Catie Rosemurgy

Love, with Trees and Lightning

I've been thinking about what love is for.
Not the dramatic part where he gathers
until he is as purposeful inside her
as an electric storm. Not when he breaks
into a thanks so bright it leaves her split
like a tree. (How we all jolt back, our picnic
ten shades lighter, our hands clapped over awe
that is too big for our mouths, our raw hearts
more tender now that they're a little burned.)
No, not the connecting and charring part.
(After all, nothing we like to call lightning
stays very long among the branches.)
But the two of them, afterwards, tasting
the electricity. Nibbling the charge
on the ions. When her soul has already
risked coming to meet him at the wide open
window of her skin. When what is left
of his body still feels huge, and he sits draped
in his fine, long coat of animal muscles
but uses all this strength to be human
and almost imperceptible. They curl up,
make their bodies the same size, draw promises
in one another's juices. "You," they say.
I love it when they say that.
Would that they could give a solid reason.
Sometimes they even refuse to try. They make jokes
while cinching their laces—"I'll call soon,"
"You are so sweet." The rank sugar of his breath
doesn't summarize the world for her. "Not you," they say.
And nothing bad has happened. They just turn
the doorknob that has been shining in their hands
the whole time, walk out, and continue to die.
Same as the rest of us. So maybe love

is a form of crying. Of finishing
what autumn leaves always start and turning
a brilliant color before we drift down.
Name one living thing that doesn't
somehow bloom. None of them get to choose
the right conditions. Think of fire, of orchids.
She's already up the street when he feels
his body pale, close, and become insufficient.
"If you go," he says out the door, "I go too."
There is no one like him, but she has no hope
of ever proving it. Instead she stays up
pressing old secrets into his skin and asking
if it hurts. He sets her on top of himself
so he can't leave without her and confesses
to feeling as if he almost matters,
as if he no longer disappears
as soon as he connects with something
receptive on the ground. She says she will
split in half for him a million times.
They bring flowers and carpet and children
into the act, stand by one another's side
for years. They refuse to move, ever. They act
as if they've found the only hospitable
spot on earth. I love it when they do that.

Prageeta Sharma

Dear _____ ,

Replication: n. I cannot dream of losing you so I will answer to your gesture
until I have a word. I will utter this word again and again.
I cannot protect you or defend you. To mimic you is to dress you.
Dearest echo, please arrive here without fear but with confidence!
But I love you now because together, and more than once,
we have challenged the language of carriages.
And although I have not thought of anything new, tomorrow,
I will countersign the papers. Today, I love the horse.
Your vision has walked loosely onto the ranch.
We think together, we copy each other. Reach for a narrow-necked bottle
bent, identical, and silver.
There, I have written you, twice.

Yours,

_____

Me in Paradise

Oh, to be ready for it, unfucked, ever-fucked.
To have only one critical eye that never
divides a flaw from its lesson.

To play without shame. To be a woman
who feels only the pleasure of being used
and who reanimates the user's

anguished release in a land
for the future to relish, to buy
new tights for, to parade in fishboats.

To scare up hope without fear of hope,
not holding the hole, I will catch
the superbullet in my throat

and feel its astounding force
with admiration. Absorbing its kind
of glory. I must be someone

with very short arms to have lost you,
to be checking the windows
of the pawnshop renting space in my head,

which pounds with all the clarity
of a policeman on my southernmost door.
To wish and not jinx it: to wish

and not fish for it: to wish and forget it.
To ratchet myself up with hot liquid
and find a true surprise.

Prowling the living room for the lightning,
just one more shock,
to bring my slow purity back.

To miss you without being so damn cold
all the time. To hold you without dying otherwise.
To die without losing death as an alternative.

To explode with flesh, without collapse.
To feel sick in my skeleton, in all the serious
confetti of my cells, and know why.

Loving you has made me so scandalously
beautiful. To give myself to everyone but you.
To luck out of you. To make any other mistake.

James Shea

Haiku

Upon Kissing You after You Vomited.
Upon Walking You Home and You Pissing
in Your Pants. Upon Asking a Complete Stranger
about Our Situation. Upon Reading Issa's
Prescripts "Issa in a State of Illness"
"At Being Bewildered on Waking" and Realizing
the Haiku Poets Were Not So Laconic and How
Could They Be? Poem Before Dying. Poem
Shortly Before I Head to Dinner. Poem in Which
I Enter Drops of Dew Like a Man with Tiny Keys.
Hitomaro has a poem called On Seeing
the Body of a Man Lying among the Stones
on the Island of Samine in Sanuki Province.
Kanyu's short poem is called A Poem
Shown to My Niece Sonsho on Reaching
the Barrier of the Ran after Being Relegated
to an Inferior Position. Poem Louis Aragon
Would Be Proud Of. Poem I'll Never Show You.
Poem Written in a Bugs Bunny Cartoon as the
Plane's Controls Come Off in My Hands. Poem
that Jerks Around Like a Hamster in a Bag. Basho
wrote a haiku for his students that he claimed
was his death poem. The night before
he said that for the last 20 years every poem
he had written had been his death poem. Upon
No Longer Recalling My Thoughts When I Was a Boy
Within My Father's Stare. At Being Exhausted
at Having to Explain Why Using Slang
Is More Fun than Reading a Dictionary of Slang.
The poet Saikaku once wrote 23,500 verses
in 24 hours. Basho saw Mt. Nikko and said,
"I was filled with such awe that I hesitated
to write a poem." Upon Looking Past You

into the Mattress, into the Faces of Prior Lovers.
Upon Trying to Cultivate My Inner Life While
Also Killing My Ego. On Watching
a 200 pd. Endangered Orangutan
Rape My Wife While She Shouts at Me
Not to Shoot Him. On Seeing a Blood-Shot
Spanish Boy Who Was Not Even Crying He Was So Sad
and Not Even Crying He Was So Sad. Poem
in Which I Embody a Moment So Vividly, So
Succinctly, Yet Decorate It with Such Sills,
Such Elaborations. Upon Doodling Your Name
Which Became Your Face Emerging from Day-Old
Coals. Upon Reading that Basho Believed "A Haiku
Revealing 70 to 80% of Its Subject Is Good, Yet
Those Revealing 50 to 60% Will Never Bore Us."
On Finally Leaving My Attic and Hearing English
for the First Time in 20 Years and It Sounding
Like an Animal's Cry Before It Attacks. Poem
in Response to Flying all the Way to Rome
To Meet You and Being Dumped at the Airport.
Poem about the Next Two Weeks We Spent Together.
Poem as I Sit on this Curb with My Head
in My Hands. Poem After Learning the Japanese
Word for the Simultaneous Feeling of Love
and Hatred. Poem for the Mountain at the End
of My Street. Poem in Response to Some of My
Recent Poems that Seem to Have Been Written
Inside an Aquarium. On Spending a Week in Silence
at a Monastery and Not Being Allowed Pen or Paper.
On Meditating and Feeling Like I Was a Blue Flame.
On Getting Up and Scribbling Something in the Bathroom.
On Stopping at the Train Tracks and Having a Deer
Break His Head Through My Passenger Window,
Stare at Me, and Then Run Back into the Wood.

Reginald Shepherd

ALSO LOVE YOU
for Chris

I think of you when I am dead, the way rocks
think of earthworms and oak roots, tendrils
that break them down to loam and nutrients,
something growing out of every
disappearance. I will be simpler then, sheer
molecule, much easier to understand:
steam rising from sidewalk vents, rain
accumulating on ailanthus leaves
after the rain has ended, the lingering smell
of rain and rotting leaves. *(Look for me,*
I'll be around, that's every song: I'll be that
too.) I will you kites unraveled from their tangled lines
(so far up you can't tell what they want to imitate),
weather balloons and evening stars, easily
mistaken objects of luminosity; observation
satellites to record you just out of sight
and tell you what you've missed. I will be
the lichen bubbling from a crack in the
Belmont Rocks, where you don't go,
between the brilliant men loitering
in their temporary beauty. You will. I will
you every artificial slab that makes a beach
if you think hard enough, anchored
fronds of blue-green algae bobbing
in the surface motion just like kelp
weaving in waves on Long Island Sound,
like, come to think of it, sirens' hair combed out
to tourmaline and emerald. I could be this fallen
branch across your path in Lincoln Park, marker: grasp it
and push it aside. I will you people bicycling
just past sunset and joggers straying from
their path, whole evenings of various exercise,

and this first of a whole series of lampposts
burned out, blocks of them. I will be the wind
that messes up your hair, you've just
gotten it cut, pollen, pawn of light and
light winds, air sultry and somehow
sexual, those men still sunning themselves,
giving themselves up to light and passing
eyes, your eyes perhaps. I'll be the things
left behind for you, I'll be much kinder
then. I'll kiss the drowsing atmosphere
all a summer's afternoon, and that's not all.

Union Square

Whether to approach from the North or South
into what failed state
on my way
                        to meet you,
crossing the square by whichever means we reach it

There is sound which passes through me, I am
a small column
in the street translucent,
I saw spaces between people,
mirrored pillars released from myself,
none is mine, no key
to the tuneless air

The trees resolve into
wildness,   are they content
                        with their moment
absolved of sky
never in the least wretched

                  To be struck by your choice

                  Manic in their blue bubble the branches

I have a key to one door in this city
and my job is to carry it around.
My long appointment comes,
what I'd been longing
to say

I lack conviction, disappear in the grass,
am terraced

in levels of disbelief
but not faithless

I came to the city where you were.

In the palm of the park
in the palm of your city
such stillness before rain—
my movements don't make a ripple
    and why did I believe this painting
    a portal for speaking with you—

No door
but a painting a wall a window and where
I had written myself into it—
the leaves in your hand, a skylight
talking to a painting
I know no better than you
      what happened

If we will be pulled apart
after a quiet drink in the lobby
by joy
borrowing a ladder
even joy
has to borrow
to know where you are

The wet marble stairs
    the stairs
orthodox bells ringing the square in sound
colored inside with fantastic blues
communicative and mute, moving
strange or internal like standing
live in presence of
an architectural understanding or love
like that of a painting. A painting.
Too grasping when I wanted
to throw open a curtain,
erotic when I meant to lay on top of the sheet

cool after a shower.
        The leaves could speak it
waving close as they do then tearing away
with wind as their excuse.

And I walked out to be plastered over with leaves
like a very weak superhero
who's forgotten the trick

        Will you see it
          on the wall of my torso in sleep,
flickering across the blades of one
shoulder or another

You in the bright street and for a minute
stopped, you were looking
at a bracelet abandoned on a step,
my view of you
deliciously occluded by the smoke from the incense man's table
does it seem like he's just one incense man though
        I am sure
        there are many
           but you
are singular and missed by me and here at last

faith too is a kind of enclosure
or is it
a gate

but for a moment I shied off
to watch you in the world, oblivious to
the way it opens
        just for you, buildings
        on the sunny side listing
to eavesdrop on your slightly bowlegged walk
I watched your head rise,
and the corners of your mouth
        myself becoming physically condensed
        so much so I
looked down to see what was happening in there
and you smelled like honey a little and yesterday's shirt

Spencer Short

ROMANTICISM

Fog heaved in like a headache only more ambitious.
The crane there. The wrecking ball with the one thought
it holds over all of our heads like

that moment in Whitman where it all breaks down,
ego/epic/subject/object, just that litany of
death death death death death wheeled out from
the storehouse of the subconscious,

nothing but the smallest strophic pebbles proffered
as offering along the windowsill. Which is one way of cheating
our tutelary gods. Part of me thinks kissing X in the park

among the belted trees another. The lashed & struck.
All of those diverging paths, Kenneth Koch's apartment towering
over us & no softball game to be found anywhere among
the bag lunches, the systolic thwack & scuffle

from the tennis courts. Our shaky administration
already suffering its final hours but what can you do?
The world's burning & lost in its burning.

Not even the ghost of a pulse, blue lips & yet
you go on pressing palm to chest, palm to chest, listening
for breath. Now the leaves enacting their strange vorticist twists.
Now the buildings with their semaphore of light.

How poetic to be young & losing one's love
in New York autumn though not the hangover.
Not the long drive home through the numinous tollbooths

& toxic correlative of industrial New Jersey. Subject,
object, ego. The cruelty with which the industrious, necessary

little ants of our despair burn so crisply beneath
the Romantic magnifying glass of language,

a little carbon-smudge of nothing where
once there was firm exoskeleton, a stern work ethic.
Though Keats might disagree & who am I to argue

with John Keats? 1795-1821. Of the bloody pillow.
Death & Eros. Part doomed genius, part sickly little brother.
Sometimes I think my worry violates all jurisdiction
as when imagining her going to fetch

something Classical from her car amid the multilingual
skitter & scree of 2 a.m. I feel a panic in my knees like
just before the crash. Other times it's enough

just to read Keats's letters, drink a beer,
watch the yard slip quietly into its petticoat of darkness:
how in the one to his brother the soul emerges only
after great effort & even then along a steady

dialectic of loss & more loss, each of us
perambulating our own dim forest of predatory grandmothers
& invidious wolves, our bread crumbs eaten hours ago

in a moment of now-embarrassing weakness.
Which explains, I think, the kiss. Her in the restaurant yelling.
To fully understand this, first you must write the paper
entitled: "Dialectics of Naivete & Nostalgia:

The Birth of the Soul in Whitman & Keats" which
will be presented at one, at three, & after the buffet. First you must
negotiate the Cliffs of Low-Spirits with sails tattered

& ablaze. Reduce. Reuse. Recycle. Certain ideas
should be avoided: the surprise visit after months of

not talking, clematis in hand or no. The spontaneous
proposal of marriage or its corollary,

the sudden desire to disrupt a marriage by (a) bomb threats,
or (b) the banging of fists on church windows. Either of which
may be found in some combination with (c) the hysterical

screaming of your intended's name into a vast &
seedless night. There are many forms of love. Of which,
these are not the best. I love you as a sheriff searches for a walnut
writes Kenneth Koch in "To You" & though I don't know

who he's talking about I believe him like I believe
the walnut is the key to a crime in which we've all been implicated.
It's terrible sometimes, this completion through subtraction.

The eddies, the wreckage, the things remembered.
The glints & glimpses. On the street, the smell of souvlaki
mixing with the rain. And in the park, wet grass,
mist rising from the mouths of small dogs.

Heaven

What was it I saw at the top
of the world as I fell
asleep last night?

Cats arguing on the rough roof

The instant those fiery lilies let go
a handful of flame petals dropped
to the kitchen floor   & the men & the women begin

the war of the orchids
The land of politeness inside my head said

you occult deep notion of nothing
you average spiritual manhood you
sachems of molasses, you hidden national will
you fractals, splintering powwows of disorder
you ladder in the meadow
up which I climb in pointed shoes

Listen:

There is a great lake called Pleasure
the color of your eyes and nestled
in the bay—

Out of black rock:
a fresh-water trickle

Juliana Spahr

WRITE LIKE ONE WALKS

I confess I was walking towards [you]
in that northern or southern or eastern or western direction.
Now I am stopped.
So this is what Sara Delano Roosevelt Park looks like.
Nothing.
I also confess I am writing this to [you]
but I am keeping it vague so I don't have to rewrite it next time I need a
        valentine, come February.
Walking here I noticed there were three turtles stacked on top of each
        other in the pet store window.
At least they all had [relation] to one another.
It has taken me many months to appreciate my new city because it took
        me away from [relation].
And still I am a little off.
Someone was playing a trumpet out the car window the other day and I
        thought, is this all this place has to offer.
When I should have been thinking,
        all right boy. It is a day worthy of a really loud trumpet.
Here in the city of Sara Delano Roosevelt Park there are many things.
A [you] is here.
A [love] for others is here.
I imagine I feel the intensity of my friends all over me.
This is about walking, or about [nothing].
I like it that way.
The way I like talking when I've drunk too much and everyone else has
        too so it doesn't matter what I say.
I like speaking in nonsense.
I like this park,
this nowhere, this two streets meeting, this three turtles, this four
        directions.

Chris Stroffolino

LOVE AS FEAR OF LOVE IN LAUGHTER

The external promise is also internal.
Just to let you know I know and now
we can move on to other things,
a change, an opposite. The external
threat that's not internal is the external
threat I will do my best to keep out.
I have built the wall. I am convinced
everyone else has too. And I want to expose
those who deny it for the liars or fools they are
because you have to think you're being laughed at first
in order to realize I'm only laughing at myself
and I want to meet you in laughter
more than I want to meet you in love
because there can be no love without laughter
or there can, but I will not meet you there.
It is the external enemy, if it brings music
I may make an exception but music's a form of laughter,
or a promise cloud I strike from
the drunken before disguised—in threat—as after.

Michael Teig

When the Time Comes

There were nights too when only a radish
lit up the room. I wanted you with me.

I pressed my face to the window
and acres of corn pressed back.

The company was dazzling:
ants, beekeepers, dignitaries

a legion of tiny gowns spinning
like parachutes in a hazy ballroom.

It went on like this for years.
I made room for you in bed.

I authored entire encyclopedias
devoted to foreplay. For example,

train tracks in the moonlight are a kind of zipper,
history has its way with us. Forgive me.

I spent too much time thinking,
I mean drinking.

I know when the time comes
I'll take my body off like a hat,

drift out past slatted houses
festooned with light,

past trees nodding at the river's edge
and all those small farms and field mice.

I'll come back to you. I'll come back
like a little girl up reading a book.

She drops an eyelash on each page.
She makes a wish and listens for morning.
I'd come back like her.

Jeff Tweedy

Prayer #3

I have pondered
the long unpublished poems
of someone's only son
that dead laugh
spun over stone
where french-kissed teenaged girls blush
and flash teasing tooth-pouts
lasting moments less
than real hope stirring
symphonic shouts
again slack
in service of dread,
mocked continents drifting
stems already shooting
across time's seamlessness
I have enjoyed these hours more
with you not by my side

Karen Volkman

FROM SPAR

When kiss spells contradiction it spills an ocean of open clothes. I gave me to one who hung hearts so high it was a mast in mute blue weather, the clang and strop of it, the undercover wet. Said are they sails your impenetrables that only winds can jibe them, the arc and the rip and the rush of all that flood. But his were slow words, more a storm than a sending, what his hands knew of tack and tumble I will not tell.

If kiss were conquest, were conclusion, I might be true. In the bluebit, heartquit leaping I might be binded. But tongue, lip, lap are brim beginning, a prank of yet. I waxed for a man all hum and hover and stuttered must, what he'd read of snowlight and sunder I'll never pearl. I said, are they moons, that they bleach in your fingers, and so much wrack at the socket, and rune and run. (Like a moon he was sharp when new and blunt when done.)

If kiss were question, were caution. What he knew of. Trice and tender. I'll never. *None.*

Catherine Wagner

LOVER

Prince Genji was in love with me in the eleventh century. Put his hand through my screens. Why Lady Murasaki you may go.

Sir Walter Scott courted me wi' glove and ring, wi' brotch and knife. I said you faker.

Sartre I fucked, it was bad.

Djuna Barnes was in love with me I told her I was scared she said Lie down!

Byron said he was we only flirted.

Will you said Lady Mary Wortley Montague stay after tea. Your ankle my dear as you rose from the clavichord.

Your hair being of the softest brightness and your bosom of the brightest softness I am loath to choose between and must address myself to both—so Philip Sidney

Once sat on Wystan Auden's lap—kissed his jaw and rubbed his belly. I stuck my hand in his pants and found his old thing. We were both delighted. "Hag," he said.

Job I said God punish you for a righteous man I am raw.

Come in while I dress. I will not, said Charlotte Brontë and waited in the snow.

Virginia W and I bathing—neglected pond. A honeybee pricked my lower thigh. Quoth she, where the bee suck—

Meredith Walters

Spontaneous Monument

On a street clogged with chatter, young men and women
saunter in their casual regalia. I carry the scent of the treeless suburbs,
deliver myself to the ranging antelopes, the four-story pair of jeans
     encased in safety glass
in case somebody goes at it with a hammer. We might think that each
     other could not resist, we think that we have never resisted the allure
of an actual response—to see or to be seen and considered,
companioning ourselves to strangers,
imagining for him a sorrow and a memory of your light-inflected bed:
a shadow pools in the throat of his arm
and your arm lifted to block the sun, these bodies being
engines of song we do not know that we remember.
Your song recalls to me the difference
between the bird and the call of the bird, and how I have failed to distinguish
each act of compassion—an anonymous bouquet
of roses that marks the final embodied moments of someone who could
     have been me,
I lead myself to believe, almost ceremonially. Romance abides
in our ideas of death but upon our passing out of memory the
nonaffiliated eavesdroppers
shall swarm the cafes, seduced by the idea that they might belong to
     anyone—
the Japanese one and the one from New Jersey who jumps when his phone
     rings.
There are believers
for whom all hopes of an after life are buried in code, as if you could tell by
     looking
where virtue resides: a woman, all women, a man who crosses the
terrain of his country on foot and carrying only a proposal of marriage.
In the name of the actual
I have journeyed to the rotunda of the exchange commission to listen for word
of the next round up. Spirited beneath my jacket:
the last indigenous songbird to resist group processing. There are no

       minutes revolving
parallel to our work and studied leisures,
no monuments to the mind in sandaled feet. No rest.
I am faithless and in love.

Karen Weiser

FROM A ROOM TO SHARE

How can the day arrest
discrete sections of objects
like plants underbreath or dreams underwater?

To say you
are watching my skin and I am
watching you is to say there transpired

my pulse in that moment
the city is heat around us
the push in that moment is inward:

when we tear apart our boxes the muted essences
seep out and grow bright, hovering there
can turn your mottled definitions

like noise disturbed water
a simple intake of air
such a light center—

for example, the things we love about
our lovers are what is different,
maybe from a linear idea of parts

the belly or back curving so,
the breast's presence in space,
an absence of chin how

these parts move together and moor
an afternoon in detail, contain a familiar identity
it follows fomenting a sound, vibration,

hum about me at great distances is wild
and flapping in silence about the apartment.

Joe Wenderoth

JANUARY 11, 1997

I love a lady's bottom. The family objects. The family says this love
will mean the end of them. *What are they,* that this love could mean the
end of them? A lady's bottom is as inevitable as it is lovable. Are we to
conclude, then, that the universe is designed to threaten the family?
Are we to believe that a lady's bottom is, in truth, a threat? In truth, the
family is a threat, and love has cowered too long.

LOVED ONE

You were not gone
but asleep through the slide show,

and you were gone
the projector pointing skyward

the ceiling quivering
with our faces.

Are there many sizes of infinity?
These are stars, this the black

tank, circular glass,
a worldless plankton,

which are *leave,*
a worldless plankton,

which are *come.*
Wake now. O mountains

O upside down mountains of light.
A brick sings like a robin.

A brick screeches like a jay.
A waltz interred by the wind.

Something moves with me,
the bonfires draw back

their ever smaller
curtains of smoke.

There *are* many sizes of infinity
and only one will do,

the one that moans a little
as I slide the slipper on.

There were mists.
A waterfall fainted

across my shoulders.
Many houses

in the valley at night
and yours was where

I stopped.

WITHOUT PITY

To embark sleepily
being everywhere
(radiant)
To fashion oneself
wholly after dogs
to talk oneself out of
a beautiful illness
eschewing affection
and envying lilies
How were the fish eaten
the fire carried
if beauty came
only by restraint
How does a ghost eat?
Even Mary crumbled under piety—
her stone son
Understanding misery
never to desert it

What can be forgiven
of its dangerous body
(not a constant)
To find the branch
of an underground river
while tongues wag out
the weakest things
To escape design
(its "higher calling")
To make or love
anything
To hate the agony
of any human thing

Rebecca Wolff

FLAME ON

Every time I approach this borrowed hearth I see the face
of the one I love. In the fire? No—maybe
in the log, on fire? Or is it in the action of the log,
thrown into the fire, that I briefly catch a glimpse of his visage?
It's so romantic, kneeling here, I wonder why
I don't just stay all day. His whole body,
riddled with inference, stretching out atop
the fevered flames.

I walk to the fireplace in performance of a function,
in perpetuity. What is triggered
by noon—the sun, spreading over the ribs
of the room, defers its gloomy dominion—in the back
of the brain is an installation; a vision: a whole room
filled with observers—an audience—on site, glued
to the spectacle of me, returning once more, then again, to my spot
on the hearth, whence I throw a switch.
The light blazes on, electrified, conducive, evocative
motion of the mind. He just barely scratches the surface.

Venice, Unaccompanied

Waking
on the train, I thought
we were attacked

by light:
chrome-winged birds
hatching from the lagoon.

That first day
the buoys were all
that made the harbor

bearable:
pennies sewn into a hemline.
Later I learned to live in it,

to walk
through the alien city—
a beekeepers habit—

with fierce light
clinging to my head and hands.
Treated as gently as every

other guest—
each house's barbed antennae
trawling for any kind

of weather—
still I sobbed in a glass box
on an unswept street

with the last
few lire ticking like fleas
off my phonecard *I'm sorry*

I can't
stand this, which
one of us do you love?

Kevin Young

LITANY

The dirt grows up
around us, dear,
the dank & the way down

of it. The day.
Once I was
in love. Once I would not say

or could not, the under
that awaits.
Today, I say over

your one name,
sound
that sole gravity.

———

The old draw-
bridge, rusted, is always up

———

North, New
London—we cross
ourselves & the river

into the past—
the submarine
memorial for those lost

at sea, sunk
miles under—the docks dry—
the rust & mist

———

Count me among the missing

———

The apples
have not kept

their promises,
grown rotten

& ran, skins
bled into brown

———

I come to your town
fog clinging to bridges
to the baring branches

———

In the calamitous city
in the songs & sinners
among the thousand throngs

I barter & belong. Out
of the coward's tooth
& arms of ocean

out of sheer
contrariness
I continue. Keep watch.

———

Hunger has me
by the belly

———

Why does the waiting
scare you & me
the silence that surrounds

it, us, this life—

I am inside this
stone you call
a city. I am king

of the gypsies.

Thin throne air.
No crown to speak of.
My body

dying, divine.

———

The day will, I know,
come—not now—
but soon & they will say

you are gone

Will I know it by
the lack of breath
—mine—the long grief
in the trees

Or will it be you
they tell of me—sickened,
stiffened, through.
Do not

worry. Will be
me beside the foot
of your bed, nothing

haunting, just
a hint. A wish.
Think

of me & breathe!
say over
again my many

my million names.

Ten Questions for Mona

I'm sitting at the same table again, in the hopes.
This time I'm sitting where you were.
Like a fragrance you had stayed to rise,

having felt just long enough under your hat,
wanting exactly what you want.
Like a fragrance you had strayed.

There are masculine and feminine willows
moving about this room.
Just now tiny machines manufacture noises

devoting themselves to the removal
and the placing. Tiny machines
manufacture noises producing

in me a feeling of productivity.
Just now a shadow
approached from the west door spilling

a glance upon me, sorry, I thought
it was you sitting down in the place
where your hands shook as you poured

evening's sweet wine out in photographs.
I watched you grow older in the approach.
Summers are loose and feathery

in consequence as a high school, or a time,
or a camp in which Right Now is a time.
You say you think of it in a good way,

in the long approach, i.e. laughter
and lightness and etcetera time
of staying too long and leaving too soon,

sitting across from you, that absolute
conditional you sitting down in the place
where I had been a glance upon me.

Right Now is a time. A child needs
to be moved less fearfully
than thinking of something else.

What flower do you bring a flower?
I'd curl up in the wrist, but there's a cat
already named there for luck and howling.

What flower do you bring a trouble?
In the course of a sleeping farther away
dawn grew your hair.

I watched you grow younger.
When I look up you will be across from me.
This time I'm sitting where you were.

Andrew Zawacki

Vertigo

If wind that wastes its time among the trees
escapes itself, only to end up quarantined
by a derelict squall from the north,

and if the air turns somersaults, miming
the outtakes of dusk, scandaled by an early frost
and punished for its coldness by the cold—

then, like a bullet that lodges in bone,
becoming a piece of the body,
you will not awake apart from your name.

And I will not be not a part of you.

———

There are things I would settle
with myself. Why, for instance,
as autumn unravels, I cannot mortar

myself to myself, nothing but sunlight
littered from here to the sun. By I
I mean a window, redness grazing the lake

at dawn, or an echo winnowing out
along a wall, hard pressed to hide itself
and straining for the voice it vanished from.

I mean so many windows. So much red.

———

Please do not misunderstand.
That woman who carries winter
inside her, dizzied by snowfall

that won't level off—I would say
I love her, but I is too strong a word
and love not strong enough.

Rachel Zucker

A Kind of Catastrophe

        about this snow I'd say
little,
        less than necessary,
                it's so
readily available for metaphor or
        melting

is not the same as
        transcendence, transformation,
    erosion—
not sure what it means,
who we might be without these
        forms
define us whether or not we willingly
conform, assert some
        desperate arrogance—

        and speaking of moons: I don't believe,
necessarily, there was one:

        for example;

. . . when the narrator says he's lost
consciousness or is dreaming of
his mother maybe
his first memory his
birth—I tend to doubt
his hazy reportage.

He says *and now a word about . . .*
but obviously means more than one.

He says *a fake ceiling* and means
a real ceiling made out of something
other than what other ceilings are made out of.

> *The snow is not going anywhere*

doesn't mean it isn't coming down and
even if I knew what color   exactly
the sky blanked out to doesn't mean
I'd tell you
        or could tell you
except by way of saying
                something
else—saying something
        close to what I mean—
something,
        not like a mirror to my soul
and not like looking *at* but seeing
        the backing painted not plated
silver, worthless, altogether—

        this doesn't mean I don't remember—

        (the snow a window the child we did not conceive that night
        I saw you then this is another winter that's still my picture
        the harsher elements and our beginning or starting to love
        and love)
                you

probably remember it differently.

Whose place is it to say what happened?

The snow is not a symbol but literal.

You happened
            and happen to be here—
    where I am
    which changes and is always,
from my point of view, first person.

I'm not the narrator or speaker,
        make a mess of omens:

                This snow

doesn't mean anything;

        I suppose you're sleeping and may be seeing
something else entirely
                    or nothing—

sometimes, you say
        don't make too much of it.

It is just snow.

            I try putting lilacs in your dream
        but can't be sure you'll see them;
            they're so far out of season,
                    I can't make them make sense.

About this snow I'd say

you're sleeping and are as beautiful this night
           as that night and that night and
that night in New Haven

      when the snow came down
and I didn't make too much of it—
         was—   we were,

          in it
        the moment
               I made a picture of
             to look at later—

      now
  you're different—   here—

                    (I never imagined)

               three winters later—

Contributors' Notes

JOSHUA BECKMAN was born October 31, 1971 in New Haven, Connecticut. He is the author of *Things Are Happening* (Copper Canyon, 1998), *Something I Expected to Be Different* (Verse Press, 2001), *Your Time Has Come* (2004) and two collaborations with Matthew Rohrer: *Nice Hat. Thanks.* (2002) and *Adventures While Preaching the Gospel of Beauty* (2003). He lives in Staten Island, New York.

JOSH BELL was born May 12, 1971. He is the author of *No Planets Strike* (Zoo Press, 2004). He was the University of Wisconsin's Diane Middlebrook Fellow for 2003-04 and the University of Iowa's Paul Engle Fellow for 2000-01. He is currently a Ph.D. Candidate in English at the University of Cincinnati.

DAVID BERMAN was born January 4, 1967 in Williamsburg, Virginia. He is the author of *Actual Air* (Open City Books, 1999) and lives in Nashville, Tennessee.

ANSELM BERRIGAN was born August 14, 1972. He is the author of *Zero Star Hotel* (2002) and *Integrity & Dramatic Life* (1999), both published by Edge Books. He lives in New York City, where he currently works as the Artistic Director of The Poetry Project at St. Mark's Church-in-the-Bowery.

EDMUND BERRIGAN was born August 3, 1974. He is the author of *Disarming Matter* (The Owl Press, 1999), as well as several chapbooks, most recently *There's No* (Angry Dog Press, 2003). He writes and performs music as I Feel Tractor, and recently released a self-titled 7" record (Loudmouth Collective, 2003). He was raised on the Lower East Side of Manhattan and now resides in Bushwick, New York.

MARK BIBBINS was born October 14, 1968. He is the author of *Sky Lounge* (Graywolf Press, 2003), which received a Lambda Literary Award. He teaches at The New School, where he co-founded *LIT* magazine, and at Purchase College. He lives in New York City.

BRIAN BLANCHFIELD was born October 5, 1973. He is the author of *Not Even Then* (University of California Press, 2004) and teaches creative writing at the Pratt Institute of Art. He lives in Brooklyn and sometimes Tucson.

LEE ANN BROWN was born October 11, 1963. She is the author of *Polyverse* (Sun & Moon Press, 1999), which won the New American Poetry Series, and *The Sleep That Changed Everything* (Wesleyan University Press, 2003). She lives in New York City and teaches poetry and literature at St. John's University.

ONI BUCHANAN was born in Hershey, Pennsylvania on March 9, 1975. She attended the Iowa Writers' Workshop for an MFA degree in poetry and recently completed a Master's degree in Music (piano performance) at the New England Conservatory of Music. Her first book of poetry is *What Animal* (University of Georgia Press, 2003). She currently lives in Boston, Massachusetts.

STEPHEN BURT was born January 6, 1971. He grew up in and around Washington, DC and currently teaches at Macalester College in St. Paul, Minnesota. His first book of poems, *Popular Music,* won the Colorado Prize for 1999; his second book of poems, *Parallel Play,* will be published by Graywolf Press in 2006.

GARRETT CAPLES was born May 25, 1972. He is the author of *The Garrett Caples Reader* (Black Square Editions, 1999) and *er, um* (Meritage Press, 2002), a limited edition collaboration with Chinese artist Hu Xin. He lives in Oakland, California.

ROBERT N. CASPER was born September 18, 1970. He is the publisher of *jubilat* and the co-founder of the *jubilat*/Jones reading series. He lives in Brooklyn, New York and works at the Council of Literary Magazines and Presses.

MICHAEL EARL CRAIG is the author of *Can You Relax in My House* (Fence Books, 2001). He currently lives with his wife Susan near Livingston, Montana, where he works as a farrier.

CAROLINE CRUMPACKER was born May 29, 1964. She is a poetry editor at *Fence* and a contributing editor for Doublechange.com. She curates a series of bilingual poetry readings at the Bowery Poetry Club and lives in Brooklyn, New York.

CYNTHIA CRUZ was born January 27, 1968 and raised in Germany and California. Her poems have appeared in *The Paris Review, Boston Review, Grand Street,* and elsewhere. She lives in New York City where she teaches at The New School and Queens College.

TENAYA DARLINGTON was born December 4, 1971. She is the author of *Madame Deluxe* (Coffee House Press, 2000), winner of the National Poetry Series. Her novel, *Maybe Baby,* was published by Little, Brown, in August 2004. She works as a journalist in Madison, Wisconsin.

CORT DAY was born November 3, 1961. He is the author of *The Chime* (Alice James Books, 2001) and is currently working on a second book, titled *Zoon.*

MÓNICA DE LA TORRE was born August 22, 1969. She is co-author of *Appendices, Illustrations and Notes* (Smart Art Press, 1999), translator of the collection *Poems/ Poemas* by Gerardo Deniz (Lost Roads, 2001), and co-editor with Michael Wiegers of *Reversible Monuments: Contemporary Mexican Poetry* (Copper Canyon, 2002).

TIMOTHY DONNELLY was born June 3, 1969. He is the author of *Twenty-seven Props for a Production of Eine Lebenszeit* (Grove Press, 2003). He has been a poetry editor at *Boston Review* since 1996 and is currently a graduate student in English at Princeton University.

BEN DOYLE was born June 11, 1973. His first book *Radio, Radio* (Louisiana State University, 2001) won the 2000 Walt Whitman Award. He has taught at the University of Iowa, West Virginia University, and Denison University.

MARCELLA DURAND was born November 17, 1967. She is the author of *Western Capital Rhapsodies* (Faux Press, 2001). She lives in New York City with her husband, painter Richard O'Russa. She is currently co-editing an anthology of contemporary French poetry, forthcoming from Talisman House in 2005, and putting the finishing touches on a new manuscript, titled *Area*.

THOMAS SAYERS ELLIS was born October 5, 1963. He is the author of *The Maverick Room* (Graywolf Press, 2005) and *The Genuine Negro Hero* (Kent State University Press, 2001). He teaches in the English Department at Case Western Reserve University and in the Low-Residency MFA in Creative Writing Program at Lesley University.

MONICA FERRELL was born November 8, 1975. She is a 2002-2004 Wallace Stegner Fellow and a former "Discovery/*The Nation*" winner. Her poems have appeared in *American Letters & Commentary, Boston Review, Fence,* and elsewhere.

THALIA FIELD was born April 4, 1966. Her collection *Point and Line* will be joined by *Incarnate: Story Material* from New Directions (2000, 2004). Her book *ULULU (Clown Shrapnel)* is forthcoming from Coffee House Press in 2005. She currently serves on the creative writing faculty of Brown University.

NICK FLYNN was born in 1960. He is the author of *Some Ether* (Graywolf Press, 2000), *Blind Huber* (2002), and *Another Bullshit Night in Suck City: A Memoir* (W. W. Norton, 2004).

GRAHAM FOUST was born August 25, 1970. He is the author of *As in Every Deafness* (Flood Editions, 2003) and *Leave the Room to Itself* (Ahsahta Press, 2003). A graduate of Beloit College, George Mason University, and the University at Buffalo, he teaches in the English Department at Drake University and lives in Iowa City, Iowa.

PETER GIZZI was born August 7, 1959. His most recent book, *Some Values of Landscape and Weather,* was published in Fall 2003 by Wesleyan University Press. Other books include *Artificial Heart* (Burning Deck, 1998) and *Periplum* (Avec, 1992).

ARIELLE GREENBERG was born October 24, 1972. She is the author of *Given* (Verse Press, 2002). She is an editor at *Court Green,* a literary annual published at Columbia College Chicago, where she is a core faculty member of the poetry program. She lives in Evanston, Illinois.

SASKIA HAMILTON was born May 5, 1967. She is the author of *As for Dream* (Graywolf Press, 2001) and *Divide These* (2005), and is also the editor of *The Letters of Robert Lowell* (Farrar, Straus & Giroux, 2005). She lives in New York City.

MATTHEA HARVEY was born September 3, 1973. She is the author of *Sad Little Breathing Machine* (Graywolf Press, 2004) and *Pity the Bathtub Its Forced Embrace of the Human Form* (Alice James Books, 2000). She is the poetry editor of *American Letters & Commentary* and lives in Brooklyn, New York.

CHRISTIAN HAWKEY was born September 14, 1969. His first book of poems, *The Book of Funnels,* was recently published by Verse Press. He lives in Fort Greene, Brooklyn.

TERRANCE HAYES was born November 18, 1971. He is the author of *Muscular Music* (Tia Chucha, 1999) and *Hip Logic* (Penguin Books, 2002). His third book, *Wind in a Box,* is forthcoming from Penguin in 2005. He lives in Pittsburgh, Pennsylvania.

STEVE HEALEY was born July 14, 1966. He lives in Minneapolis, Minnesota, where he teaches writing to prisoners in several Minnesota Correctional Facilities. His first book of poems is *Earthling* (Coffee House Press, 2004).

BRIAN HENRY was born September 17, 1972. He is the author of three books of poetry, *Astronaut* (Carnegie Mellon, 2002), *American Incident* (Salt Publishing, 2002), and *Graft* (New Issues Press, 2003), and editor of *On James Tate* (University of Michigan, 2004). He lives in Athens, Georgia.

CHRISTINE HUME was born May 21, 1968. She is the author of *Musca Domestica* (Beacon Press, 2000), winner of the Barnard New Women Poets Prize, and *Alaskaphrenia* (New Issues Press, 2004), winner of the Green Rose Award. She teaches at Eastern Michigan University.

HENRY ISRAELI was born June 14, 1967. His books include *New Messiahs* (Four Way Books, 2002) and *Fresco: Selected Poetry of Luljeta Lleshanaku* (New Directions, 2002), which he edited and co-translated. He is also the founder of Saturnalia Books.

MAJOR JACKSON was born September 9, 1968. He is the author of *Leaving Saturn* (University of Georgia Press, 2002), which was short-listed for the National Book Critics Circle Award. He is an associate professor of English at the University of Vermont. His second book of poems, *Hoops,* is forthcoming from W. W. Norton.

LISA JARNOT was born November 26, 1967 in Buffalo, New York. She is the author of three volumes of poetry: *Black Dog Songs* (Flood Editions, 2003), *Ring of Fire* (Zoland Books, 2001; Salt Publishing, 2003), and *Some Other Kind of Mission* (Burning Deck, 1996). Her biography of the poet Robert Duncan, *The Ambassador from Venus,* is forthcoming from the University of California Press in 2005.

DEVIN JOHNSTON was born March 14, 1970. He is the author of two books of poetry, *Aversions* (Omnidawn, 2004) and *Telepathy* (Paper Bark Press, 2001), and has also published a book of criticism, *Precipitations: Contemporary American Poetry as Occult Practice* (Wesleyan University Press, 2002). With Michael O'Leary, he publishes Flood Editions. He lives in St. Louis, Missouri.

W. B. KECKLER was born January 3, 1966. His books include *Sanskrit of the Body* (Penguin Books, 2002), winner of the National Poetry Series, *Ants Dissolve in Moonlight* (Fugue State Press, 1995), and *Recombinant Image Day* (Broken Boulder Press). He lives in Harrisburg, Pennsylvania.

JOANNA KLINK was born July 15, 1969. She teaches at the University of Montana and is the author of *They Are Sleeping* (University of Georgia Press, 2000). She is currently working on a second book of poems, *Circadian.*

NOELLE KOCOT was born November 14, 1969. She is the author of *4* (Four Way Books, 2001), *The Raving Fortune* (2004), and *Poem for the End of Time and Other Poems* (2006). She lives in Brooklyn, where she was born and raised.

AARON KUNIN was born in 1973 and lives in Connecticut. His poems have appeared in *No: A Journal of the Arts, Fence, Radical Society,* and elsewhere.

CHRISTIAN LANGWORTHY was born January 12, 1967. He has published widely in anthologies and journals such as *Michigan Quarterly Review, Failbetter,* and *Can We Have Our Ball Back?*

TANYA LARKIN was born November 30, 1972. She lives in Somerville, Massachusetts and teaches creative writing and English at The New England Institute of Art. "Cho-Fu-Sa" was written for Joanna Hershon and Derek Buckner on the occasion of their wedding in 1999.

KATY LEDERER was born in 1972. She is the author of the poetry collection *Winter Sex* (Verse Press, 2002) and the memoir *Poker Face* (Crown, 2003). She lives in Brooklyn, New York, where she edits her own magazine, *Explosive.*

LISA LUBASCH was born March 13, 1973. She is the author of *To Tell the Lamp* (Avec Books, 2004), as well as *Vicinities* (2001) and *How Many More of Them Are You?* (1999). Her translation of Paul Éluard's *A Moral Lesson* is forthcoming from Green Integer Books. She lives in New York City and is an editor of Doublechange.com.

SARAH MANGUSO was born February 12, 1974. She is the author of *The Captain Lands in Paradise* (Alice James Books, 2002). With Jordan Davis, she is co-editor of the anthology *Free Radicals: American Poets Before Their First Books* (Subpress, 2004). She teaches at The New School.

ROSS MARTIN was born November 29, 1973. He is Head of Programming for MTVU. He has taught at Washington University, Rhode Island School of Design, and The New School. Zoo Press published his first book, *The Cop Who Rides Alone,* in 2001.

CATE MARVIN was born November 20, 1969. Her first book, *World's Tallest Disaster* (Sarabande Books, 2001), was selected by Robert Pinsky for the 2000 Kathryn A. Morton Prize. Currently she is an assistant professor in creative writing at the College of Staten Island CUNY.

ANTHONY MCCANN was born September 13, 1969 and raised in Columbia and Rensselaer Counties in New York state. He is the author of *Father of Noise* (Fence Books, 2003). He teaches English as a Second Language in Brooklyn, New York, where he lives with his wife.

AARON MCCOLLOUGH was born April 15, 1971 and raised in Tennessee. His first collection of poems, *Welkin,* won the 2002 Sawtooth Poetry Prize and was published by Ahsahta Press. His second collection of poems, *Double Venus,* was published by Salt Publishing in 2003. He edits the online literary journal GutCult (www.gutcult.com).

JEFFREY MCDANIEL was born July 3, 1967, and raised in Philadelphia. He is the author of *The Splinter Factory* (Manic D Press, 2002), *The Forgiveness Parade* (1998), and *Alibi School* (1995). He teaches at Sarah Lawrence College.

MARK MCMORRIS was born April 10, 1960. He is the author of *The Cafe at Light* (Roof Books, 2004), *The Blaze of the Poui* (University of Georgia Press, 2003), *The Black Reeds* (1997), and other volumes of poetry. He is an associate professor of English at Georgetown University in Washington, DC.

RICHARD MEIER was born May 8, 1966. His first book, *Terrain Vague,* was selected by Tomaž Šalamun as winner of the Verse Prize and published by Verse Press in 2000. He is currently Visiting Assistant Professor of English at Beloit College.

LYNN MELNICK was born November 11, 1973. Her poems have appeared in *Boston Review, CROWD, Denver Quarterly, The Paris Review,* and elsewhere. She lives in Brooklyn, New York.

CHELSEY MINNIS was born March 16, 1970. She is the author of *Zirconia* (Fence Books, 2001), which was the winner of the Alberta Prize. She is currently working on her second book titled *Bad Bad.* She lives in Denver, Colorado.

ANGE MLINKO was born September 19, 1969. She is the author of *Matinées* (Zoland Books, 1999) and the forthcoming *A Book Called Odile.* She lives in Brooklyn, New York.

JENNIFER MOXLEY was born May 12, 1964. She is the author of *Imagination Verses* (Tender Buttons, 1996) and *The Sense Record and other poems* (Edge Books, 2002). She lives in Orono, Maine, and works as an assistant professor at the University of Maine.

MAGGIE NELSON was born March 12, 1973. Her books of poems include *Shiner* (Hanging Loose, 2001), *The Latest Winter* (2003) and *Jane: An Investigation in Poems* (Soft Skull Press, 2005). She currently teaches at Wesleyan University.

DANIEL NESTER was born February 29, 1968. He is the author of *God Save My Queen* (Soft Skull Press, 2003) and *God Save My Queen II* (2004). His work has appeared in *Open City, Nerve, LIT,* and *The Best American Poetry 2003.* He lives with the love of his life, Maisie Weissman.

HOA NGUYEN was born January 26, 1967 and lives in Austin, Texas, with her husband, the poet Dale Smith. Together they edit *Skanky Possum,* a journal and book imprint. Her book of poems, *Your Ancient See Through,* was published by Subpress in 2002.

TRAVIS NICHOLS was born March 26, 1979. He is in love with the poet Monica Fambrough. They live together in Massachusetts.

GEOFFREY NUTTER was born April 28, 1968. He is originally from Sacramento, California and was educated at San Francisco State University and the University of Iowa. He is the author of *A Summer Evening* (Center for Literary Publishing, 2001). He lives in New York City with his wife and daughter.

G. E. PATTERSON was born in the middle of the country and grew up along the Mississippi River.

ETHAN PAQUIN was born March 16, 1975. He is the author of *Accumulus* (Salt Publishing, 2003), *The Makeshift* (Stride Publications, 2002), and *The Violence* (Ahsahta Press, 2005). He edits *Slope* and Slope Editions from Buffalo, New York, where he teaches at Medaille College.

D. A. POWELL was born May 16, 1963 and is the author of *Cocktails* (Graywolf

Press, 2004), *Lunch* (Wesleyan University Press, 2000) and *Tea* (1998). Together with Katherine Swiggart, he edits the online magazine *Electronic Poetry Review* (www.poetry.org).

KEVIN PRUFER was born October 22, 1969. He is the author of *Strange Wood* (Louisiana State University, 1996), *The Finger Bone* (Carnegie Mellon, 2002), and *Fallen from a Chariot* (2005). He is the editor of *Pleiades: A Journal of New Writing* and lives in Warrensburg, Missouri.

HEATHER RAMSDELL is the author of *Lost Wax* (University of Illinois Press, 1998), which won the National Poetry Series. A founding member of the Brooklyn Drama Club, she co-created the play *The Situation Room.* Her writing has appeared in *An Anthology of New (American) Poets* (Talisman House) and *American Poetry: The Next Generation* (Carnegie Mellon University Press). She lives in Brooklyn and Cambridge.

CLAUDIA RANKINE was born September 4, 1963. She is the author of four collections of poetry: *Don't Let Me Be Lonely* (Graywolf Press, 2004), *Plot* (Grove Press, 2001), *The End of the Alphabet* (Grove Press, 1998) and *Nothing in Nature is Private* (CSU Poetry Center, 1995). She is co-editor, with Juliana Spahr, of *American Women Poets in the 21st Century* (Wesleyan University Press, 2002).

SRIKANTH REDDY was born May 1, 1973. He is the author of *Facts for Visitors* (University of California Press, 2004). He is currently the Moody Poet-in-Residence at the University of Chicago.

PAM REHM was born October 21, 1967. She is the author of *Gone to Earth* (Flood Editions, 2001), *To Give it Up* (Sun & Moon Press, 1995), and other collections. She lives in New York City.

PETER RICHARDS was born July 13, 1967. He is the author of *Nude Siren* (2003) and *Oubliette* (2001), both from Verse Press. He is the Briggs-Copeland Lecturer in Poetry at Harvard University.

ELIZABETH ROBINSON was born December 3, 1961. She is the author of 6 books of poetry, most recently *Pure Descent* (Sun & Moon Press, 2003), a National Poetry Series winner, and *Apprehend,* winner of the Fence Modern Poets Series. She recently moved to Boulder to teach at the University of Colorado.

MATTHEW ROHRER was born February 9, 1970. He is the author of *A Hummock in the Malookas,* winner of the 1994 National Poetry Series and published by W. W. Norton, *A Green Light* (Verse Press, 2004), *Satellite* (2001), and two collaborations with Joshua Beckman: *Nice Hat. Thanks.* (2002) and *Adventures While Preaching the Gospel of Beauty* (2003). He lives in Brooklyn and is an editor for Fence Books.

CATIE ROSEMURGY was born December 3, 1969. She is the author of *My Favorite Apocalypse* (Graywolf Press, 2001). She teaches creative writing at The College of New Jersey.

PRAGEETA SHARMA was born February 5, 1972. She is the author of *Bliss to Fill* (Subpress, 2000) and *The Opening Question* (Fence Books, 2004). She lives in Brooklyn, New York.

BRENDA SHAUGHNESSY was born March 21, 1970. She is the author of *Interior with Sudden Joy* (Farrar, Straus & Giroux, 1999). Recently she has been a Bunting Fellow at the Radcliffe Institute for Advanced Study at Harvard University and a Japan/U.S. Friendship Commission Fellow. She lives in Brooklyn, New York.

JAMES SHEA was born April 27, 1976. He studied at the University of Iowa and Utsunomiya University, Japan. He currently teaches at DePaul University and Columbia College Chicago.

REGINALD SHEPHERD was born April 10, 1963. He is the editor of *The Iowa Anthology of New American Poetries*, forthcoming from the University of Iowa Press, and the author of *Otherhood* (University of Pittsburgh, 2003), *Wrong* (1999), *Angel, Interrupted* (1996), and *Some Are Drowning* (1994). He currently lives with his partner in Pensacola, Florida.

LORI SHINE was born June 21, 1975. Her poems have appeared in *Boston Review, The Canary, Conduit, CROWD,* and other magazines. She lives in western Massachusetts.

SPENCER SHORT was born October 4, 1972 in Elkton, Maryland. His first book, *Tremolo,* was published by HarperCollins in 2001. He is currently a student at the University of Chicago Law School.

ELENI SIKELIANOS was born May 31, 1965. Her most recent books of poems are *The Monster Lives of Boys & Girls* (Green Integer, 2003), winner of the National Poetry Series, and *Earliest Worlds* (Coffee House Press, 2001). *The California Poem* (Coffee House), and *The Book of Jon* (City Lights) will both be published in Fall 2004. She lives and teaches in Colorado.

JULIANA SPAHR was born April 7, 1966. She is the author of *Fuck You-Aloha-I Love You* (Wesleyan University Press, 2001), *Response,* (Sun & Moon Press, 1996), a winner of the National Poetry Series, and numerous chapbooks. She is also co-editor, with Claudia Rankine, of *American Women Poets in the 21st Century* (Wesleyan University Press, 2002). She currently teaches English at Mills College in California.

CHRIS STROFFOLINO was born March 20, 1963. He may not know what love is, but he is the author of three books of poetry, including *Speculative Primitive* (Tougher Disguises Press, 2005) and is the singer/songwriter and keyboardist for Continuous Peasant (www.continuouspeasant.com).

MICHAEL TEIG was born April 22, 1968. Currently he lives in Massachusetts, where he works as a freelance writer and editor. His first book, *Big Back Yard,* was the winner of BOA Editions' inaugural A. Poulin Jr. Poetry Prize in 2003. He is also a co-founder and a co-editor of *jubilat.*

JEFF TWEEDY was born in 1967. He has dedicated the last twenty years of his life to being a songwriter and musician, currently for the popular music band Wilco, and formerly of the band Uncle Tupelo. He lives in Chicago, Illinois with his wife and two sons.

KAREN VOLKMAN was born in Miami on January 18, 1967. Her two books are *Crash's Law* (W. W. Norton, 1996), and *Spar* (University of Iowa Press, 2002), which received the James Laughlin Award. She currently teaches in the MFA program at the University of Montana.

CATHERINE WAGNER was born in 1969. She is the author of *Macular Hole* (Fence Books, 2004), *Miss America* (2001), and many chapbooks, including the recent *Imitating* (Leafe Press, 2004), and *Exercises* (811 Books, 2003). She is poetry editor of *Radical Society* and lives and teaches in Boise, Idaho.

MEREDITH WALTERS was born January 23, 1973. She is a curator of education at the Walker Art Center in Minneapolis, Minnesota. She is a native of Hampton, Virginia.

KAREN WEISER was born August 27, 1975. She is the author of the chapbooks *Placefullness* (Ugly Duckling Presse, 2004) and *Eight Positive Trees* (Pressed Wafer, 2002). She lives in New York City where she is studying for her doctorate in English.

JOE WENDEROTH is the author of *Letters to Wendy's* (Verse Press, 2000), *It Is If I Speak* (Wesleyan University Press, 2000), and *Disfortune* (1995).

SAM WHITE was born January 24, 1973. He is a writer and illustrator and lives in Providence, Rhode Island.

ELIZABETH WILLIS was born April 28, 1961. She is the author of *Turneresque* (Burning Deck, 2003), *The Human Abstract* (Penguin, 1995), and a book-length poem, *Second Law* (Avenue B, 1993). She currently teaches at Wesleyan University.

REBECCA WOLFF was born November 29, 1967. She is the editor and publisher of *Fence* and Fence Books. She is the author of *Manderley* (University of Illinois, 2001) and *Figment* (W. W. Norton, 2004). She lives somewhere with her husband and son.

MONICA YOUN was born May 5, 1971. Her first book of poems, *Barter*, was published by Graywolf Press in 2003. She lives in New York, where she is an entertainment lawyer.

KEVIN YOUNG was born November 8, 1970, and is the author of *Jelly Roll* (Knopf, 2003), *To Repel Ghosts* (Zoland Books, 2001), and *Most Way Home* (Zoland Books, 2000; William Morrow, 1995). He is the editor of *Giant Steps: The New Generation of African American Writers* (HarperCollins, 2000) and the Everyman's Library Pocket Poet anthology *Blues Poems* (2003).

MATTHEW ZAPRUDER was born November 22, 1967. He is the author of *American Linden* (Tupelo Press, 2002), and the editor of Verse Press.

ANDREW ZAWACKI was born May 22, 1972. He is the author of two books of poetry, *Anabranch* (Wesleyan University Press, 2004) and *By Reason of Breakings* (University of Georgia, 2002). He is coeditor of *Verse*, editor of *Afterwards: Slovenian Writing 1945–1995* (White Pine Press, 1999), and a student in the Committee on Social Thought at the University of Chicago.

RACHEL ZUCKER was born December 27, 1971. She is the author of *The Last Clear Narrative* (Wesleyan University Press, 2004) and *Eating in the Underworld* (2003). She has been married for seven years.

Editors' Acknowledgments

This anthology could never have been created without the poets and musicians who agreed to contribute to the book and CD, and we extend our most sincere thanks and appreciation. We are also indebted to the publishers for generously granting permission to use these poems, as well as to the small magazines and webzines where many of these poems first appeared.

We owe a great deal of gratitude to Matthew Zapruder for his support and enthusiasm for this anthology, from initial inception to final manuscript, as well as for curating a collection of songs to accompany the book.

We are also grateful to the Verse staff, especially Lori Shine and J. Johnson, without whom this book would have been merely a sheaf of papers; to Charles Simic, for his wonderful introduction; to Alice Quinn, the Poetry Society of America, and the Academy of American Poets; to Poets House for providing us with an annex to our own library; and to the following individuals for their conversations, advice, and guidance on so many matters, including this anthology: Joshua Beckman, Rob Casper, Timothy Donnelly, Seth Fleischman, Matthea Harvey, Jared Hayley, Stefania Heim, Jennifer Kronovet, Lynn Melnick, and Matt Rohrer.

To our wonderful families and friends, our love and deepest thanks.

———

BRETT FLETCHER LAUER was born August 15, 1978 in Philadelphia, Pennsylvania. He is the Poetry In Motion® Director at the Poetry Society of America and poetry editor of *CROWD* Magazine. He is the co-editor of *Poetry In Motion from Coast to Coast* (W. W. Norton, 2002) and his poems have appeared in *BOMB, Boston Review,* and elsewhere.

AIMEE KELLEY was born June 7, 1979. She received her BA in English from UC Berkeley and her MFA from the New School for Social Research. She is the editor and publisher of *CROWD* Magazine and has worked at nonprofit organizations such as the Council of Literary Magazines & Presses and the Academy of American Poets. Her poems have appeared in *Denver Quarterly, Spinning Jenny,* 811 Books, and elsewhere.

———

CHARLES SIMIC was born May 9, 1938, in Belgrade, Yugoslavia. He is the author of numerous books, including *Jackstraws* (Harcourt Brace, 1999), which was named a Notable Book of the Year by *The New York Times; Walking the Black Cat* (Harcourt Brace, 1996), which was a finalist for the National Book Award in poetry; *A Wedding in Hell* (1994); *Hotel Insomnia* (1992); *The World Doesn't End: Prose Poems* (1990), winner of the Pulitzer Prize for Poetry; and *Selected Poems: 1963-1983* (1990). He lives in New Hampshire, where he is Professor of English at the University of New Hampshire.

Acknowledgments: Poems

Joshua Beckman, "(Don't be mad...)" from *Your Time Has Come*. Copyright © 2004 by Joshua Beckman. Reprinted with the permission of Verse Press.

Josh Bell, "Poem to Line My Casket with, Ramona" from *No Planets Strike*. Copyright © 2004. Reprinted with the permission of Zoo Press, all rights reserved.

David Berman, "Classic Water" from *Actual Air*. Copyright © 1999 by David Berman. Reprinted with the permission of Open City Books.

Anselm Berrigan, "The various multitudes contained by the loves of my love" from *Integrity & Dramatic Life*. Copyright © 1999 by Anselm Berrigan. Reprinted with the permission of Edge Books.

Edmund Berrigan, "The History of the Human Body" from *Disarming Matter*. Copyright © 1999 by Edmund Berrigan. Reprinted with the permission of The Owl Press.

Mark Bibbins, "By the Skin of Our Luck" from *Sky Lounge*. Copyright © 2003 by Mark Bibbins. Reprinted with the permission of Graywolf Press, Saint Paul, Minnesota.

Brian Blanchfield, "The Endowment Becoming Less An Institution" from *Not Even Then*. Copyright © 2004 by The Regents of the University of California. Reprinted with the permission of the University of California Press.

Lee Ann Brown "After Sappho" from *Polyverse*. Copyright © 1999 by Lee Ann Brown. Reprinted with the permission of Sun & Moon Press/ Green Integer Books, Los Angeles.

Oni Buchanan, "The Only Yak in Batesville, Virginia" from *What Animal*. Copyright © 2003 by Oni Buchanan. Reprinted with the permission of The University of Georgia Press.

Stephen Burt, "A Sudden Rain in the Green Mountains" from *Popular Music*. Copyright © 1999 by Stephen Burt. Reprinted with the permission of the Center for Literary Publishing.

Garrett Caples, "Targets and Flowers (Begun with Lines from Breton)" from *The Garrett Caples Reader*. Copyright © 1999 by Garrett Caples. Published by Black Square Editions. Reprinted with the permission of the author.

Robert Casper, "Untitled" used with the permission of the author.

Michael Earl Craig, "Good Night, Star" from *Can You Relax In My House*. Copyright © 2002 by Michael Earl Craig. Reprinted with the permission of Fence Books.

Caroline Crumpacker, "Trans-Relational Love Poem" used with the permission of the author.

Cynthia Cruz, "Self Portrait in Horse Hair Wig" originally appeared in *The Paris Review*, Issue 169. Reprinted with the permission of the author.

Tenaya Darlington, "Field Guide to Western Intimacy" originally appeared in the *Black Warrior Review*, Volume 29, Issue 2. Copyright © 2003. Reprinted with the permission of the author.

Cort Day, "Once As Thoth Beside The Sea" orginally appeared on the Verse Press Younger American Poets Feature online. Copyright © 2002 by Cort Day. Reprinted with the permission of the author.

Mónica de la Torre, "Driven by a Strange Desire" originally appeared in *Fence*, Volume 3, Number 1. Copyright © 2000. Reprinted with the permission of the author.

Timothy Donnelly, "Isn't It Romantic?" from *Twenty-seven Props for a Production of Eine Lebenszeit*. Copyright © 2003 by Timothy Donnelly. Reprinted with the permission of Grove/Atlantic, Inc.

Ben Doyle, "An Error of the Hydrographers" is used with the permission of the author.

Acknowledgments: Music

"Only a Monster," written by Franklin Bruno. Performed by Jenny Toomey and Franklin Bruno. Copyright © 2002 Stopgap Measures Music (BMI). Used by permission of Jenny Toomey, Franklin Bruno, Stopgap Measures Music and Misra Records. From the album "Tempting: Jenny Toomey Sings the Songs of Franklin Bruno" on Misra Records.

"The Ocean Cliff Clearing (Live)," written and performed by Richard Buckner. Copyright © 1998 Richard Buckner. Used by permission of Richard Buckner.

"In My Way, Yes," written and performed by Vic Chesnutt. Copyright © 2003 Ghetto Bells Music, administered by Bug Music. Used by permission of Vic Chesnutt, Ghetto Bells Music and New West Records.

"Butterscotch," written and performed by CocoRosie. Copyright © 2004 CocoRosie Music. Used by permission of CocoRosie and Touch and Go Records.

"Downpour," written by Thane Thomsen. Performed by The Figments. Copyright © 2001 by Thane Thomsen. Used by permission.

"I'm Gonna Watch You Sleep," written and performed by Hamell on Trial. Copyright © 1999 Trial Size Publishing (ASCAP). Used by permission of Hamell on Trial and Such-A-Punch Media.

"Down the Wrong Road Both Ways," written and performed by Magnolia Electric Company. Copyright © 2004 Magnolia Electric Company. Used by permission of Jason Molina.

"Perversity," written by Matt Sutton and performed by the Malarkies. Copyright © 2000 Matt Sutton and Muss My Hair Records. Used by permission.

"Loving Pauper," performed by Doug Martsch, John Mullen, Ned Evett, and Ian Waters. Written by Dobby Dobson. Publishing information unavailable at printing. Used by permission.

"Don't Talk Crazy," written and performed by Mark Mulcahy. Copyright © 2004 Paymarx Music. Used by permission of Mark Mulcahy and Mezzotint Records.

"O My Stars," performed by Nanang Tatang. Written by Michael Hurley. Copyright © 1980 Snocko Music (BMI), administered by Bug Music. Used by permission of Nanang Tatang and Snocko Music.

"Fighting Off the Pricks," written and performed by New Radiant Storm King. Copyright © 2004 Furnace Rock (ASCAP). Used by permission of New Radiant Storm King.

"All For You," written and performed by Nina Nastasia. Copyright © 2002 Vine St. Music (BMI). Used by permission of Nina Nastasia and Touch and Go Records.

"No Other Love," written and performed by Chuck Prophet. Copyright © 2002 Kingsblood Music (BMI), administered by Bug Music. Used by permission of Chuck Prophet, Kingsblood Music and New West Records.

"She Is My Diary," written and performed by Ray's Vast Basement. Copyright © 1997, Subterranean 78's (BMI). Used by permission.

"With You," written and performed by Megan Reilly. Copyright © 2003 Fanore by the Sea. Used by permission of Megan Reilly and Carrot Top Records, Inc.

"Pretty Eyes," written by D.C. Berman. Performed by Silver Jews. Copyright © 1996 Civil Jar Music (BMI). Used by permission of Silver Jews and Drag City Records.

"Catch 22 (ver. 2)," written and performed by Spouse. Copyright © 2004 Spousemusic (ASCAP). Used by permission of Spouse and Pigeon Records.

Introduction to the CD

If, at any moment, you're one of the very few people in your city or town or rural area reading a poem, the sound of your own voice—aloud, or in your head—will happen against a kind of overwhelming silence that mocks the very act of speaking. You might hear some traffic, a radio from the next room, perhaps a conversation, maybe even a cow. But mostly silence, interrupted by someone's words just carried along by someone's voice, your own, for a while until it stops.

When you're reading a poem it's your own voice you hear alone against that silence. It's more comforting to have someone else singing to you, not to mention a little music, if also even sadder when the song is over. Of course you can just keep fooling yourself wonderfully by rewinding, and having the singer sing to you, over and over again.

Songs and poetry are like each other in as many ways as they're not. Like juggling and hang gliding, they're activities considered vaguely ridiculous, sometimes dangerous (especially if the chainsaws are on fire), and generally irrelevant. Things ok and even pretty cool if someone does them, just not your loved ones.

And surely songs and poetry try to get to that same place, the one where the listener has suddenly fallen through the trap door and into the middle of feeling something huge and new and very familiar for the first time rushing through.

Maybe so. But clearly lyrics exist in a context—i.e. melody, other instruments, quality of the voice, and so on—and have to relate to many consistent and repeating formal structures. On the other hand, nowadays most poets write in "free" verse, that is without submitting their poems to rhyme or regular meter. Which means the poem as it is being written unfolds within a terrible, exhilarating, and often for the artist debilitating freedom. Hello darkness my old friend.

To work in the context of music must create opportunities and difficulties for the songwriter who wants to communicate something meaningful or true. I imagine it's not unlike the situation that faces the poet who writes in form. To write in prescribed forms forces a poet to search out and be found by new and exhilarating ways of speaking. The danger is, if you're clever, it's easy to say something, but the more clever you are the harder it is to force yourself not just to say something that works, but something you actually care about and other people will too.

I can't speak for songwriters in general, but the ones who were generous enough to contribute to this joint project seemed genuinely happy about the idea of being in the same place as poets and poetry. Better here than a library. Maybe sometimes songwriters get sick of the idea that they aren't being taken seriously as they think poets are, in the same way poets get sick of not having anybody throw underwear at them.

What I think is this is an extraordinary collection of songs. Each of these songwriters is doing something new in an old tradition, which is more than we've been led to have any right to expect except from our most interesting and committed artists, which is who these people are. There's no reason to call them poets, any more than there is to call us poets singers, but secretly as we know we've all been on the same team all along.

Matthew Zapruder

CD Track List

1   **The Malarkies**   Perversity

2   **Vic Chesnutt**   In My Way, Yes

3   **CocoRosie**   Butterscotch

4   **Doug Martsch**   Loving Pauper

5   **Hamell on Trial**   I'm Gonna Watch You Sleep

6   **Chuck Prophet**   No Other Love

7   **New Radiant Storm King**   Fighting Off the Pricks

8   **Magnolia Electric Co.**   Down the Wrong Road Both Ways

9   **Michael Zapruder**   Blackhawk

10   **Nina Nastasia**   All For You

11   **Richard Buckner**   The Ocean Cliff Clearing (Live)

12   **Jenny Toomey and Franklin Bruno**   Only a Monster

13   **Spouse**   Catch 22 (ver.2)

14   **Nanang Tatang**   O My Stars

15   **Ray's Vast Basement**   She Is My Diary

16   **Jenny Toomey**   Pressure

17   **The Figments**   Downpour

18   **Mark Mulcahy**   Don't Talk Crazy

19   **Megan Reilly**   With You

20   **Silver Jews**   Pretty Eyes